"I'm not exaggerating when I say that I've *ever* read about the costly and ex time, *A Loving Life* is the most faithfu love for us in Jesus I've fed on in years. These two themes go the biblical story of Ruth, Paul Miller gives us hope, not hype—the freedom to suffer well, stay present, and live expectantly in all of our relationships. Thank you, Paul, for making the gospel more beautiful and believable to me."

Scotty Smith, Teacher in Residence, West End Community Church, Nashville, Tennessee

"Every once in a great while one reads a book that is so profound, so fresh, and so life changing that you can't get it out of your mind or your heart. *A Loving Life* is that kind of book. Walk with Paul Miller, Ruth, and Naomi to the place of real love, and you'll never again settle for a substitute. Read this book, rejoice in it, and give it to everyone you know. They will bless you for giving it to them as I bless Paul Miller for writing it."

Steve Brown, Host, *Key Life* radio program; author, *Three Free Sins: God Isn't Mad at You*

"If there is a message the world needs more to hear and to start obeying than the one Paul Miller brings here, I don't know what it is. Beautifully written and attested by plenty of personal experience, *A Loving Life* unearths dimensions of the book of Ruth I had never noticed, and will now never forget."

Andrée Seu Peterson, Senior Writer, *World* magazine

"The book of Ruth is about *hesed*, a loyal love, that Ruth shows to Naomi, Boaz shows to Ruth, and, behind the scenes, God demonstrates to his people. Paul Miller not only brilliantly explains the story of Ruth, but also shows how *hesed* love can transform us and our relationships. I highly recommend this book."

Tremper Longman III, Robert H. Gundry Professor of Biblical Studies, Westmont College

"Being married to Joni, a longtime quadriplegic, I know my marriage vows are always in need of polishing. And Paul Miller's new book fits the bill; I've yellow-highlighted nearly every page. *A Loving Life* reinforces that the best—the only—kind of love is one-way and without an exit strategy. If you are looking to shore up the for-better-or-for-worse, in-sickness-and-in-health promises in your marriage, you couldn't lay your hands on a better read."

Ken Tada, Director of Ministry Development, the Joni and Friends International Disability Center

"'Death is the center of love.' Miller's insight comes as he beautifully retells the story of Ruth in terms of the gospel, revealing a path of love more dear and deep than our cultural icons and distractions can create, and more precious than any pursuit of self can dream. Here is love vast, unmeasured, boundless, free, and freeing."

Bryan Chapell, President Emeritus, Covenant Theological Seminary; Senior Pastor, Grace Presbyterian Church, Peoria, Illinois

"The word *love* is often either a vague sentiment or just another four-letter word. But in Paul Miller's hands, the quiet, compelling reality emerges. You will witness how love is thoughtful, principled, courageous, enduring, and wise—all the things you know deep down it should be. And even more than those fine things, you will be surprised and delighted at how true love is grounded in God."

> **David Powlison,** faculty, Christian Counseling and Educational Foundation;
> Senior Editor, *Journal of Biblical Counseling*

"Paul Miller reminds us with boldness and insight that a relationship with Jesus Christ means journeying with him to the cross, where we most know of the love of God for us. As such, it is the only path to learning to incarnate that love ourselves—and so to dance to the Spirit's constant rhythm of being loved and loving others."

> **Joseph "Skip" Ryan,** Minister, Park Cities Presbyterian Church; Moderator,
> General Assembly of the Presbyterian Church in America

"I was sure that Paul Miller's *A Praying Life* had to be his greatest, but *A Loving Life* is better. How can we care for others much more than for ourselves? How can we escape from the slippery pit of our 'feel good' culture? Keep going through the book of Ruth and discover good and godly ordinary life, and how you can live it in an extraordinary way—the way of love, God's way."

> **D. Clair Davis,** Emeritus Professor of Church History, Westminster
> Theological Seminary

"*A Loving Life* is a worthy successor to Paul Miller's much-appreciated book on prayer. It is a careful, thorough analysis of the book of Ruth, understanding it as a love story and making good applications to our own experiences and needs for love. Paul here shows not only a deep understanding of God's Word, but also a rich knowledge of human nature, both in the ancient world and today. He offers biblical responses to many of the misunderstandings and problems we have with love of all kinds. May the Lord give this book a broad readership!"

> **John M. Frame,** J. D. Trimble Chair of Systematic Theology and Philosophy,
> Reformed Theological Seminary, Orlando, Florida

"Reading this book nourished me deeply. With caring attentiveness especially to often-overlooked 'modern' widows and widowers, Paul Miller gently pastors us through the story of two courageous, *hesed*-embracing single women, Naomi and Ruth. He invites us to embrace the death at the center of covenant love and to learn it as the downstroke of reality—the upstroke of which is ever the grace of surprising resurrection. In Christ, Christians all, and the world, reap the far-reaching blessing of these unlikely benefac-tresses. And we do again in this little book."

> **Esther L. Meek,** Professor of Philosophy, Geneva College; author, *Loving to
> Know: Introducing Covenant Epistemology*; *A Little Manual for Knowing*

A LOVING LIFE

A
LOVING
LIFE

In a WORLD *of* BROKEN
RELATIONSHIPS

Paul E. Miller
Author of *A Praying Life*

WHEATON, ILLINOIS

Dedicated to those who do *hesed* love:
Barb, Carolyn, Carren, Chris, Dan and Lisa,
David and Brooke, Denise, Dianne, Don and Linda,
Holly, Jill, Joe and Colleen, Julie, Karl and Janet,
Kate, Linda, Lisa, Lucy, Margarete, Mary, Nancy,
Paul, Philip and Susanna, Philip and Suzanne,
Ralph and Isabel, Rich and Ruth, Rob and Lynn,
Roger and Jane, Steve, Tina, and Vicki

A special *thank you* to
Ron and Kim Avery, Ray and Dianne Baker,
Howard and Deanna Bayless, David and Amy Dodd,
Jim and Cynthia Eckert, Kristina Kimball,
Greg and Marcia Riching, Steven and Tammy Scruggs,
Dwight and Jayna Smith, the Sweet and Strawbridge
families in honor of John E. Sweet, Jim and Christy Valenti,
Thomas Wilson, and Stephen and Kinsey Young
for helping make this book possible

CONTENTS

INTRODUCTION:
A LOVE-HATE RELATIONSHIP
WITH LOVE

George[1] sat across the table from me in a Chicago restaurant. Nine years ago he had been an elder at his conservative evangelical church when he'd walked away from his wife, Teresa. He told me, "I'm good at starting to love, but really bad at the follow-through." I thought Teresa would agree. I said, "So you have a love-hate relationship with love. You want intimacy, but you become overwhelmed with the work of love." George nodded.

I had contacted George on a whim. I'd known him and his wife at the time of their separation and divorce, and I'd been praying for Teresa. I was doing one of our A Praying Life seminars in Chicago and the thought had occurred to me, "Contact George." He'd texted Teresa out of the blue a couple of times during the year, hinting that he was sick of his life. I wondered if there might be an opening. Two weeks before, unknown to me, Teresa had begun to pray that God would bring godly men into George's life. When I contacted him, he agreed to meet.

I asked George why he'd left Teresa. He said, "I was overwhelmed by the black hole of her needs. I couldn't take her demanding spirit and constant criticism." I knew Teresa would not disagree—God had done a work in her since the divorce. I thought there was no point in beating around the bush: "George, at the heart of love is incarnation that leads to death. Death is at the center of love. It happened to Jesus. It happened to us."

I took a drink of water and continued. "I discovered this twenty years ago when I immersed myself in the Gospels, the story of Jesus's life. This understanding of love transformed how I related to people."

I knew George was puzzled by what I was saying, but I wanted to give him a map for the future. I wanted him to know that there was at least one person in the world who thought it was possible to endure in love. I wanted to give him hope.

I was praying my way through the meeting, unsure of what to say. Sure enough, George asked me, "What does Teresa think of me?" I had nothing to lose, so I said, "George, you lack three things: purity, integrity, and endurance." He didn't disagree. He told me that the night before, he'd slept with a woman he barely knew. Though saddened, I was heartened by his honesty. It was a step in the direction of integrity.

Beginning a Journey of Love

George had inhaled the spirit of the age. He'd been chasing his feelings and desires instead of doing the good work of love. His last long-term relationship had broken up, and he'd been devastated. He was alone now, and he hated it.

I wanted George to understand what love looked like, so I said, "Before sleeping with that woman last night, you went on a path with her. The two of you went through a kind of dance. You were both kidding yourselves, but it was still a mini-journey. All of us are on journeys, regardless of whether the journey is characterized by self or love. The Hebrews thought of a life of love not as just a state, but as a path of righteousness, a direction."[2]

George leaned toward me as I talked. I sensed that it was providing a new frame for him to think about his life. So I continued, "Satan wants us to view our life in isolation, as disconnected from any path. For example, Vegas's marketing slogan, 'What happens in Vegas, stays in Vegas.' You can come to Vegas, have anonymous sex, and return home as if nothing happened. Of course, that's a bunch of baloney. Vegas changes you. We bring Vegas back home in our hearts. Everything we are doing is creating the persons we are becoming. Our life is a trajectory."

I invited George to join me on a pilgrimage of learning to love. I invite you to do the same. We learn to love not abstractly, but on the journey itself. On a journey we lock ourselves into a specific, physical path. So in this book we're going to lock ourselves into the Bible's story of Ruth and Naomi as they make this journey of love. On the way, we'll discover not only love but ourselves as well. Learning to love is inseparable from coming alive as a person, from seeing our own hearts, and how the siren song of the age seduces us.

From Dreams to Disaster

George's self-reflection "I'm good at starting to love, but bad at the follow-through" reflects our culture. We start well but end badly. Because of our culture's debt to Christianity and its resurrection hope, we are a culture that dreams big about love.

No place dreams better than Disney. The promise of Disney—marriage happily ever after—dominates the popular mind of our age. It is a good but unrealistic dream. When God is removed from the dream, the story turns out badly. Christianity without Jesus just doesn't work. The Disney dream raises unrealistic expectations and then dashes them on the rocks of human frailty. Naive expectations make us high maintenance and supersensitive. Human frailty makes us cynical, doubting the possibility of love. The new American journey is from naiveté to cynicism. The result? We feel abused, betrayed, and bitter. It was better not to have dreamed. The magic is gone.

As our culture loses its Christian moorings and searches for new myths, for new ways of making sense of life, it is lurching back to the world of paganism—the world before Christianity—where "everyone did what was right in his own eyes" (Judg. 21:25). That quote describes the time of the judges, which is the setting of the book of Ruth. Ruth begins with, "In the days when judges ruled . . ." (Ruth 1:1). A modern paraphrase for our culture might be, "In the days of Oprah when *feelings* ruled. . . ." Oprah has an amazing ability to empathize with people, but she, along with most of our cultural elites, channels nineteenth-century thinkers like Emerson and Thoreau who made feelings and self-actualization absolute. "How I feel" or "my happiness" is the new standard.

George used the language of feelings to do what he felt like. He told Teresa when he left her, "I'm not happy and marriage is not for me. I grew up, and I got tired of it all." The false hope of Disney combined with following his feelings had shaped George's behavior and given him a false trajectory or path to follow. The result? Not only was George lost, but Teresa was discarded.

Thousands of modern "widows" and "widowers" find themselves in similar straits: the spouse stuck in a loveless marriage with a harsh and demanding partner; the young woman who has offered herself to a man without the protection of a committed relationship and now finds herself abandoned; the young woman searching in vain for a young man to love her—with so many men enmeshed by the listless, commitment-phobic spirit of our age.

Whatever the source of the broken relationship, the result remains the same—the loneliness of a fairy tale gone bad. What do you do when you are abandoned by your husband? How do you survive when no matter how much love you pour into your wife, she becomes more demanding? How do you endure in love? How do you endure without love when you long to get married? How do you keep your spirit from shutting down?

To these modern widows and widowers, I write this book—to encourage you, to give you a hope and a future. We'll pursue that by joining two ancient widows, Ruth and Naomi, on their journey. The book of Ruth is an ideal narrative for our post-Christian world, where breaking covenants—not enduring in love—is the new norm. Ruth offers a template for love that understands both the craziness of our modern world and a way forward. Ruth is all about surviving and even thriving in a collapsing world.

Enjoying the Beauty

I hope the book of Ruth affects you the way a trip to the Grand Canyon or Chartres Cathedral near Paris might. How do you *apply* the Grand Canyon or Chartres? Of course, you don't *apply* the Grand Canyon—you are stunned by the beauty. You don't *apply* Chartres—you worship there. You stop talking as you let it fill your soul. You are silent as your soul expands. You sense that you don't have enough capacity to capture the beauty—the experience of entering and beholding beauty is too much.

It takes time to travel to the Grand Canyon or Chartres. So be patient with the historical background laced throughout the book. As we follow the story of Ruth and Naomi, we are entering a different world from our own, going back 3100 years to 1100 BC and what historians call Iron Age I. But when we pause to understand the cultural and language differences, we'll discover that people are the same.

Because we'll discover different aspects of love as we encounter them in the story of Ruth, our journey, like all good journeys, will have a meandering quality to it. But that's part of the fun of pilgrimage. Our journey follows the book of Ruth, building like a Bach fugue, simple at first, almost plain, then growing gradually more complex as the following themes emerge:

- *Love.* What is love? What is the cost of love? Why do we shy away from love? What does it mean to love when you get no love in return?
- *Gospel.* How does understanding the love that we see in the book of Ruth enrich and anticipate our understanding of the gospel, of God's love for us? How is the gospel a journey?
- *Community.* How do we create community? What is the glue that keeps us together?
- *Lament.* How do you relate to God when he seems to have deserted you? How does faith encourage us to lament? Why do we dislike the idea of a lament?
- *Prayer.* What does a praying life look like? Do we wait for God to act or do we act? What does it mean to live in a story?
- *Femininity.* What does it mean to be feminine? How do we survive and even thrive in a world (as this one was) dominated by men?
- *Masculinity.* What does a godly man look like? What characterizes him? How do you combine gentleness and power?

The story of Ruth can transform you if you allow it to remap your own story and draw you into a life of love. In a world that is losing its capacity to feed our souls, I hope that the book of Ruth fills your soul, and then overflows into your life.

Part One

COMMITTED LOVE

SUFFERING:
THE CRUCIBLE FOR LOVE

Suffering is the crucible for love. We don't learn how to love anywhere else. Don't misunderstand; suffering doesn't create love, but it is a hothouse where love can emerge. Why is that? The great barrier to love is ego, the life of the self. In long-term suffering, if you don't give in to self-pity, slowly, almost imperceptibly, self dies. This death of self offers ideal growing conditions for love. So, not surprisingly, this book on love, the book of Ruth, begins with the descent of Naomi's family into a crucible of suffering.

Naomi had a dream. It was a simple dream of a husband, children, and grandchildren. With a few deft strokes, the narrator paints the death of that dream, the death of her entire family. Suffering sneaks up on her, tragedy on tragedy.

> In the days when the judges ruled there was a famine in the land, and a man of Bethlehem in Judah went to sojourn in the country of Moab, he and his wife and his two sons. The name of the man was Elimelech and the name of his wife Naomi, and the names of his two sons were Mahlon and Chilion. They were Ephrathites from Bethlehem in Judah. They went into the country of Moab and remained there. But Elimelech, the husband of Naomi, died, and she was left with her two sons. These took Moabite wives; the name of the one was Orpah and the name of the other Ruth. They lived there about ten years, and both Mahlon and Chilion died, so that the woman was left without her two sons and her husband. (Ruth 1:1–5)

Ancient readers would have been intrigued and possibly troubled by the family's move to Moab (see fig. 1.1). The Moabites were the hillbilly cousins of the Israelites, the result of an incestuous relationship between

Lot and one of his daughters. *Mo* means "who" and *ab* means "father." So *Moab*, reflecting its murky origin, is the land of Who's Your Daddy?[1]

Figure 1.1. Map of Moab

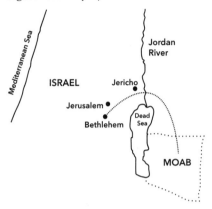

Bad blood grew between the cousins. When the Israelites tried to pass through Moab on the way to Canaan, the Moabite king opposed them by bribing the prophet Balaam to prophesy against them. When that backfired, the women of Moab seduced the Israelite men. The Israelites regularly called Kemosh, the Moabite god, "filth" or "loathsome." One day Yahweh would crush Kemosh in a pit of manure (Isa. 25:10–11). Moab meant trouble.[2] And trouble is what the family found in Moab.

Naomi's losses would be staggering for any culture, but in the ancient Near East for a mother to lose not only her husband but also her sons was the epitome of suffering. A leading management consultant posed this hypothetical situation to American men: "Your mother, your wife, and your daughter are all in a sinking boat and you can rescue only one of them. Who do you rescue?" Sixty percent would rescue their daughter and 40 percent their wife. All would leave the mother adrift. Sorry, moms. The consultant then posed the same question to Saudi men, and every one of them said they would rescue their mother. Why? In the traditional cultures of the Near East, mothers have no identity outside the home. Their daughters marry and leave while their sons remain, forging a powerful mother-son bond. Their sons are their life.[3]

Naomi has lost her life. She has entered into a living death. Where we see a sharp line between death and life, the Hebrews saw a gradation.[4] Living outside of Israel, the Promised Land, is already a partial death. Now with the death of her husband and two sons, Naomi's life is functionally over. It no longer has meaning or purpose. If you have experienced deep, sustained suffering, then you know Naomi's frame of mind. Death would be a relief. You might not commit suicide, but if your life ended you wouldn't care.

Naomi's tragedy is a series of downward steps. First Elimelech dies, but hope is not lost because her two sons find Moabite wives, and their sons could carry on the family name. But the two wives, Ruth and Orpah, are barren, so Naomi has no grandsons to carry on Elimelech's name—that is the heart of Naomi's tragedy. The death of her two sons seals that tragedy. One of the families in the oldest clan of Bethlehem, the Ephrathites, has died out.[5] So Naomi doesn't just lose her husband and two sons; she loses her future, her reason for living.

There is a remnant though. In ancient Near Eastern culture, the wife moved in with the husband's family. Daughters left home; brothers and their families stayed. Brothers lived together, even after their father died, maintaining their inheritance as common property.[6] Psalm 133 reflects how good it is when "brothers dwell in unity" (v. 1). So both Orpah and Ruth have been living with Naomi for some time. Now Naomi is left with the empty shell of a family, a fragile, highly vulnerable family. "Ruth, Orpah, and Naomi are headless. There are no husbands, no fathers, no sons to take a protective role."[7] Because of her age, Naomi is not likely to remarry. She has no trade or means of support. All exits were closed.

Where Is God?

We get an inkling of Naomi's internal struggles from the meaning of the names. Bethlehem is actually a two-word name like New York. *Beth* means "house," and *lehem* means "bread." So *Bethlehem* means "house of bread," possibly a granary or a reference to the abundance of food. Naomi's husband's name, Elimelech, means "my God is king." Naomi means "pleasant." The two sons' names are Mahlon ("weak") and Chilion ("frail").[8]

Ancient readers took names seriously.[9] If we listen like an ancient reader, this is what we hear:

In the days when the judges ruled there was a famine in the land, and a man of the *House of Bread* in Judah went to sojourn in the country of *Who's Your Daddy*, he and his wife and his two sons. The name of the man was

> *My God Is King* and the name of his wife *Pleasant*, and the names of his two
> sons were *Weak* and *Frail*. They were Ephrathites from the *House of Bread*
> in Judah. They went into the country of *Who's Your Daddy* and remained
> there. But *My God Is King*, the husband of *Pleasant*, died, and she was left
> with her two sons. These took Moabite wives; the name of the one was
> Orpah and the name of the other Ruth. They lived there about ten years,
> and both *Weak* and *Frail* died, so that the woman was left without her two
> sons and her husband.

Can you hear the irony? A famine in the *House of Bread*? *God Is King* is dead? *Pleasant's* husband and sons have died? Reality is mocking God. In other words, because Naomi hopes in God, her grief intensifies. When God does not meet our expectations, it opens the door not just to despair but also to cynicism, to shutting down our hearts with God.

Don't Flee the Crucible

Suffering is the frame, the context, where we learn to love. Sometimes it is a sucker punch—the phone call from the doctor or the note from the spouse—but most of the time it slips up on you, bit by bit, as it did Naomi and Ruth. Then comes the day when you realize that you hate your life, and you want out.

The Disney dream not only fails to prepare us for the crucible, but it also makes the crucible far worse. We come into relationships expecting the best, and often discovering the worst. The shock of encountering the ugliness of sin leaves us floundering.

We have much to learn about love from this story, but all we need to know at this point is this: you can't flee the crucible. Love will not grow if you check out and give in to the seductive call of bitterness and cynicism—or seek comfort elsewhere. We have to hang in there with the story that God has permitted in our lives. As we endure, as we keep showing up for life when it makes no sense, we learn to love, and God shows up too.

George fled the crucible. Overwhelmed by the demands of love, he set out on a false pilgrimage. He had listened to a modern myth that says, "Love is a feeling. If the feeling is gone, then love is gone." Hollywood has no resources to endure in love when the feeling is gone. Actually, that's the point when we are ready to learn how to love.

Hints of Resurrection

One of the oddest things about deep suffering is that the sun comes up in the morning. Life limps along. So after our quick thirty-thousand-feet overview, the narrator of Ruth takes us to ground level, and we watch three women, the remnants of a family, trudging along the road from Moab.

> Then she arose with her daughters-in-law to return from the country of Moab, for she had heard in the fields of Moab that the LORD had visited his people and given them food. So they set out from the place where she was with her two daughters-in-law, and they went on the way to return to the land of Judah. (Ruth 1:6–7)

Naomi and her daughters-in-law, in keeping with a wider definition of family, instinctively operate as a unit. But strikingly, Orpah and Ruth have decided to leave their families, their entire social network, and their cultures to live with their mother-in-law in a foreign land. In traditional Eastern cultures the daughter-in-law became a servant of the mother-in-law. This led to a tremendous amount of abuse. Even in the West, we joke about the mother-in-law–son-in-law relationship only because the real deal, the mother-in-law–daughter-in-law relationship, is often too painful. That Ruth and Orpah prefer their mother-in-law gives us some sense of how remarkable Naomi must be.

Naomi is doing the one thing essential for pilgrimage: she is enduring, hanging in there, literally putting one foot in front of the other as she heads back to Bethlehem. But how do you hang in there? Where do you get the power to love when you don't get any love in return? How do you face living alone? The answer is simple: hope. You can hang in there if you know the end of the story.

A glimmer of hope leads Naomi back. Yahweh ("the LORD") has visited his people. It isn't just that weather patterns have changed; God is involved. We're at ground zero of what makes love possible, of the difference between Disney and Christianity. Disney is *groundless human optimism*. The gospel is *real divine hope*—God breaking through into the story of my life, creating resurrection. This glimmer of resurrection hints of good things to come.

Teresa saw a hint of resurrection when she started praying for men to come into George's life. Two weeks later, seemingly out of the blue, I had this thought, "Contact George." We can endure in love if our God acts in time and space. Hope is critical to love.

2

LOVE WITHOUT AN EXIT STRATEGY

As the three women walk down to the Jordan River Valley, the full weight of the implications of Naomi's daughters-in-law returning with her dawns on her. The first words of a biblical character are often a clue to his or her character, and Naomi's first words are filled with a thoughtful love:[1] "But Naomi said to her two daughters-in-law, 'Go, return each of you to her mother's house. May the LORD deal kindly with you, as you have dealt with the dead and with me'" (Ruth 1:8).

Naomi begins by blessing Ruth and Orpah, by thinking about their futures. She blesses them twice. First she asks that the Lord would "deal kindly" with them. The phrase translated "deal kindly" is actually *hesed*, a word unique to Hebrew that combines "love" and "loyalty." She wants God to do *hesed* love with them.

Understanding *Hesed* Love

Sometimes *hesed* is translated "steadfast love." It combines commitment with sacrifice. *Hesed* is one-way love. Love without an exit strategy. When you love with *hesed* love, you bind yourself to the object of your love, no matter what the response is. So if the object of your love snaps at you, you still love that person. If you've had an argument with your spouse in which you were slighted or not heard, you refuse to retaliate through silence or withholding your affection. Your response to the other person is entirely independent of how that person has treated you. *Hesed* is a stubborn love.

Love like this eliminates moodiness, the touchiness that is increasingly common in people today. When my father, Jack Miller, began to observe this phenomena in the 1970s, he said, "It is like people don't have any skin. They are all nerve endings." Moodiness often begins with accumulated slights or the day just not working. Our inner spirits momentarily give up on life, and we stop caring how we affect people around us. Self is set on hair trigger. If we do *hesed*, that is no longer the case. It doesn't mean that we don't have moments and days when we have the cranks or share how fragile our spirit is; we just refuse to let it affect us. *Hesed* is opposite of the spirit of our age, which says we have to act on our feelings. *Hesed* says, "No, you act on your commitments. The feelings will follow." Love like this is unbalanced, uneven. There is nothing fair about this kind of love. But commitment-love lies at the heart of Christianity. It is Jesus's love for us at the cross, and it is to be our love for one another.

When feelings are the standard, we are left adrift on a turbulent sea. Every good feeling becomes a new path, so we become good at starting to love, but bad at finishing. Soon we are lost and alone in a maze of relationships.

When we get lost, we hunt for an escape. It is easy to appear to be doing *hesed*, when in fact you've exited a relationship emotionally. If someone has hurt you, you may slip into emotional revenge, hunting for bad news about that person or just running a magnifying glass over his or her character. Or you exit in your mind by creating or nourishing a world that doesn't exist. Guys can be drawn to porn; women to romance novels.

Because *hesed* love isn't centered on the fairness, it can reset quickly. For instance, if you've had an argument with a spouse or friend, you may be tempted to pull away, to distance yourself. Sometimes that distancing is appropriate, but more often it is a silent mini-revenge, a way of punishing the person for hurting you. But with *hesed* love, after an argument, even when tension is in the air, you don't allow your spirit to pull away. You move toward the other person; you don't allow an ugly space to grow.

Why is *hesed* love so important? Because life is moody. Feelings come and go. Pressures rise and fall. Passions ebb and flow. *Hesed* is a stake in the heart of the changing seasons of life. Words of commitment create a bond that stands against life's moodiness.

Ruth and Orpah have already been showing Naomi this one-way love. Naomi's comment suggests this: "May the LORD do *hesed* with you, as you have dealt with the dead and with me." Naomi is asking God to show them the same *hesed* that they have shown her.

Understanding Rest

But Naomi isn't finished. She has a second blessing: "The LORD grant that you may find rest, each of you in the house of her husband!" (Ruth 1:9). The Hebrew word for "rest" is *manoah* and is related to Noah. It means "a place of settled security," a place where *shalom* (peace) takes place. In a sense we are all hunting for rest.

Naomi's faith is striking. She assumes that Yahweh can bless her daughters-in-law in Moab. In the ancient world, gods were hardwired to ethnic groups and their land. Winning a war meant that "our god beat up your god." So Kemosh, the god of the Moabites, is strong in Moab but weak outside of Moab. Ancient people would assume that the same is true of Yahweh: strong in Israel but weak outside the borders. But the Hebrew Bible—along with Naomi—insists that Yahweh is not just a local deity but the God of the whole earth. He can bless even in Moab.

The Structure of Love

We can sense the strength of Naomi's character behind her kind words. She begins her double blessing with two sharp commands: "go" and "return." She is not negotiating. She is ordering. She has to be strong. She is taking the most precious thing in her life, her family, and destroying it for the sake of love. Because of her love, she has to push away what she loves the most, destroying the only thing she has left in the world, her only reason for living. She can't change her life, but she can improve the lives of her daughters-in-law. We are watching *hesed* in action.

Naomi gives Ruth and Orpah freedom, marriage, and children, and takes on her already broken life, loneliness, and poverty. By giving up what little hope she has left, she gives them a hope and a future. By deepening her own death, she offers them a reason for living. That kind of exchange anticipates Jesus's death, where he takes our sin and gives us his gift of acceptance, righteousness, and purity. Substitution is the structure of love (see fig. 2.1). That's why, subconsciously, we are allergic to love. We rightly sense that death is at the center of love.

Figure 2.1. How hesed *love works*

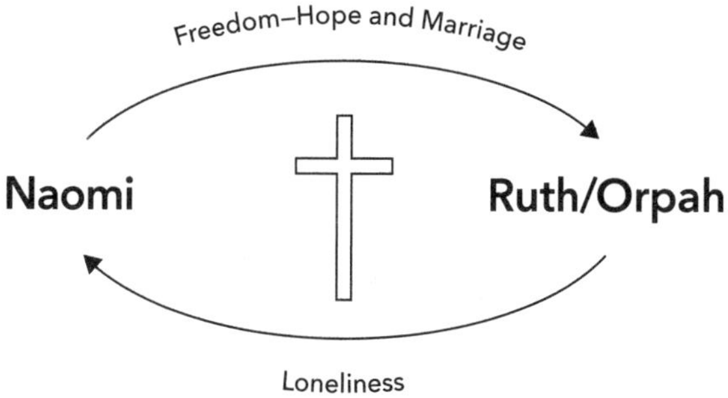

I saw my friend Joanne give up almost as much as Naomi when she invited her younger sister Shelly to live with her to protect Shelly from a sexual predator. Shelly is disabled and is naive about men. She lived with her parents, and they let her sit around and watch TV most of the day. A man who already had four children by four different women began pursuing Shelly. When Joanne got wind of this, she pled with her parents to let her take Shelly into her home. Joanne, like Naomi, begged for the privilege of narrowing and burdening her own life. When you realize that death is at the center of love, it is quietly liberating. Instead of fighting the death that comes with love, you embrace what your Father has given you. A tiny resurrection begins in your heart.

Ruth and Orpah know that Naomi is inviting even more death into her life. So when she kisses them good-bye, they respond by wailing, Eastern culture's strongest form of lament. "Then she kissed them, and they lifted up their voices and wept. And they said to her, 'No, we will return with you to your people'" (Ruth 1:9–10). The girls aren't budging. Being gracious doesn't work. So Naomi tries a new strategy in her pursuit of love.

3

THE LOST ART OF LAMENT

Naomi's initial strategy to sacrifice her own future for the sake of her daughters-in-law's future fails. Their *hesed* of her can't be broken, so she pulls out all the stops in this brilliant, grief-stricken argument:

> But Naomi said, "Turn back, my daughters; why will you go with me? Have I yet sons in my womb that they may become your husbands? Turn back, my daughters; go your way, for I am too old to have a husband. If I should say I have hope, even if I should have a husband this night and should bear sons, would you therefore wait till they were grown? Would you therefore refrain from marrying? No, my daughters . . ." (Ruth 1:11–13)

At the heart of Naomi's argument is an ancient form of Social Security called levirate marriage. If a woman's husband died, his brother was obligated to marry her, to take her as a second wife. Any children she had by him would receive her first husband's inheritance. This law not only saved a wife from famine, but provided heirs for the deceased husband and continued his name.

Naomi is implying that if she were to give birth to more sons, then she would give them to Ruth and Orpah as husbands. But Naomi is not pregnant, and she is too old to have children. She brings home her point by sketching out an incredible, multilevel miracle. If she were to (1) get married that night and (2) become pregnant with (3) twin (4) boys (5) on her wedding night, it would still be too long for Ruth and Orpah to wait. Ruth and Orpah are likely in their late twenties. If they were to wait another eighteen years for the hypothetical miracle boys to grow up, they would be in their midforties, too old to have children and with their lives mostly gone.

Naomi answers her own question as to whether they would wait with an emphatic "Absolutely not!" She paints a situation as bleak as possible in order to help Ruth and Orpah see how hopeless their situation would be with her. "Face the facts. I'm as good as dead."

Making the case so strongly with her daughters forces Naomi to think about how awful her own life is. Her heart breaks and grief pours out: "No, my daughters, for it is more bitter for me than you that the hand of the LORD has gone out against me" (1:13).[1] To drive home the point that they should not come with her, she passionately reminds her daughters-in-law how bitter her life is—more bitter than theirs. They have both lost their husbands, but they are young and can remarry. Hope is not lost. But Naomi has no hope. She is telling them, "My life is over. Yours doesn't have to be." Naomi literally says in the Hebrew, "for the hand of Yahweh went out against me." Her only conclusion is that "Yahweh's own hand has attacked me!"[2] Libbie Groves puts it this way:

> Naomi is an Israelite, one of Yahweh's own children, and yet his hand has persecuted her. There is deep, ancient, forever-binding covenantal anguish in her complaint. Yahweh is her God, and yet he is against her. He has not only allowed but orchestrated the mini-holocaust of which she is the sole survivor, left destitute and without hope. That hurts! You might expect to be treated badly by some stranger, but not by your dad.[3]

What Can We Say to Naomi's Lament?

Naomi makes us, with our Western cultural roots, a little nervous with her seeming disrespect of God. Yes, her life is hard, but should she blame God? Her open passion sends shivers down our stoic-tuned religious sensibilities, and we instinctively clamp down with our theology and say, "Naomi, God is orchestrating this. He's in control. Don't blame him." Her grief and anger unsettle us and open doors to unbelief in our own lives. We'd rather quiet her with good theology. We think we're comforting her, but maybe we're trying to keep our own demons in place.

How does God respond to her accusations? In the context of the whole book of Ruth, Ruth's love is God's response to Naomi's lament.

COMMITTED LOVE

God often uses human agents to show his love. So God weeps with her: "Then they lifted up their voices and wept again" (Ruth 1:14).

I remember many years ago at a pastors' conference, a pastor opened up his heart and shared his struggles with cynicism and unbelief. He lamented, "What about me? What do I do with my heart?" The other pastors began offering advice—all except one young missionary. He was so troubled, he interrupted them and said, "Our brother doesn't need advice; he needs someone to weep with him." Then he burst into tears and prayed for the struggling pastor. It transformed the conference.

What can we say to Naomi's lament? Nothing. Absolutely nothing. We just weep with her. That is good theology, to weep with those that weep. God does not lecture Naomi. Nor should we lecture those who are grieving. It is a striking example of Jesus's command to "judge not" (Matt. 7:1). Oddly enough, good theology drives Naomi's frustration with God. She feels anguish precisely *because* she believes God is in control. In contrast, paganism resigns itself to the hand that fate deals us.

It is easy to have the wrong kind of resignation to suffering. In *A Praying Life* I tell the story of how our daughter Kim would pace in the early morning because of her autism. My wife, Jill, would yell at Kim to go back to bed, and I would ignore Kim, just trying to get some sleep. On the surface, Jill's yelling seems less spiritual than my silence, but the opposite is true. Jill was passionately engaged with something that wasn't working. I shut it out. God can work with the former, not the latter. He can work with something that is moving, but not when our head is (literally) under the pillow. In fact, it was only because Jill yelled that I finally began to pray with Kim regularly.

In the West, we've lost the practice of lamenting. In contrast, the ancient Hebrews were constantly in God's face. About one third of the Psalms are laments where the psalmists pour out their hearts to God. Listen to these Hebrew laments:

> Why, O Lord, do you stand far away?
> Why do you hide yourself in times of trouble? (Ps. 10:1)

> How long, O Lord? Will you forget me forever?
> How long will you hide your face from me? (Ps.13:1)

My God, my God, why have you forsaken me?
  Why are you so far from saving me, from the words of my groaning?
    (Ps. 22:1)

How long, O Lord, will you look on? (Ps. 35:17)

O Lord, why do you make us wander from your ways
  and harden our heart, so that we fear you not? (Isa. 63:17)

Such honesty seldom characterizes our praying. Our inability to lament is primarily due to the influence of the Greek mind on the early church. Greek Stoicism believed that emotions—anything that interrupted the goal of a calm and balanced life—were bad. The passionate person was the immature person. Balance was everything. Naomi's brokenness feels unbalanced, so instinctively we want to correct her tilt.

A lament grieves that the world is unbalanced. It grieves at the gap between reality and God's promise. It believes in a God who is there, who can act in time and space. It doesn't drift into cynicism or unbelief, but engages God passionately with what's wrong.

When God didn't seem to be answering her prayers for Kim, Jill started praying her Social Security number because it seemed like God didn't know who she was. That's a lament with a Philly twist!

Imagine if George had been able to lament when he faced his wife's demanding spirit: "God, I don't know how to live with my wife. She's driving me crazy. It feels like I'm entering a black hole to listen to her." A lament is a prayer, a plea for help. No one can endure the weight of *hesed* love alone. An honest lament makes *hesed* love possible.

At the same time, Naomi's lament turns inward. Her genuine faith and deep love combine with hints of bitterness ("God has attacked me") and self-pity ("it is more bitter for me than you").[4] Absent in her lament is any recognition that her family might have erred in leaving Bethlehem. God is the only one at fault. We'll discover later that the narrator suggests that the return to Bethlehem was a kind of repentance on Naomi's part. Instinctively, we like neat categories of saint or sinner. But like many of us, Naomi is ambiguous.

Accepting ambiguity is immensely helpful in the work of love, because when we encounter this strange mixture of good and bad in

COMMITTED LOVE

another person, we tend to lock onto the evil and miss the good. We don't like ambiguity. We prefer the clarity of judging.

The Cost of Love

Naomi's conversation with her daughters-in-law goes through three phases. She begins by warmly but firmly directing them home. When they refuse, she paints a bleak picture of her future, laying out the hopelessness of her situation with cold logic. Finally, the grief that has pierced her soul comes to the surface. But even in her grief Naomi uses her anguish to care for Ruth and Orpah, saying in effect, "Do you really want to be around someone whom God has attacked?"

Look how painful this conversation is for Naomi. Her daughters-in-law don't brush off easily because they had bound themselves to her in *hesed* love. So Naomi is forced by her *hesed* of them to become firmer. In other words, their love for her deepens her agony. She is forced to make her hopeless life even worse by pushing away the two people dearest to her. Naomi is correct. Her life is indeed bitter.

Ironically, Naomi has to get rid of what is left of the skeleton of her family for the sake of love. The very act of love tears her apart. She is cutting off her leg to save their lives. She is broken by love.

That is *hesed* in action, death at the center of love. C. S. Lewis captures Naomi's grief perfectly:

> There is no safe investment. To love at all is to be vulnerable. Love anything, and your heart will certainly be wrung and possibly broken. If you want to be sure of keeping it intact, you must give your heart to no one, not even to an animal. Wrap it carefully round with hobbies and little luxuries; avoid all entanglements; lock it up safe in the casket or coffin of your selfishness. But in that casket—safe, dark, motionless, airless—it will change. It will not be broken; it will become unbreakable, impenetrable, irredeemable. . . . The only place outside Heaven where you can be perfectly safe from all the dangers and perturbations of love is Hell.[5]

Ruth and Orpah do not debate Naomi, because she is right. The first time Naomi initiated kissing them good-bye, but this time, "Orpah kissed her mother-in-law." Overcome by Naomi's logic, Orpah leaves for home.

Far from the bitter old woman she is usually portrayed as, Naomi is a woman of heroic love who is broken by life. She loves in the midst of tragedy—there is no greater test of character. She doesn't turn inward and take care of herself. Nor is she a two-dimensional, plastic saint. She loves with wisdom and boldness, even courage.

Loving against My Feelings

A good friend of mine, Debbie, was told by her husband, Robert, "I don't have any feelings for you anymore so I'm leaving." When I heard this, I thought, "Really? And what spouse doesn't feel that multiple times in his or her marriage?" Because it didn't feel good, Robert walked away from a thirty-year-old marriage commitment.

Like Robert, Naomi felt and articulated the full weight of her broken life. Life was so bad that it felt like the Lord himself had attacked her as an enemy. It felt like she had been abused by a seemingly loving Father. But unlike Robert, Naomi didn't let those feelings trap her. She felt her anguish, yet she was free from the tyranny of her feelings.

Debbie's life was shattered by Robert's rejection of her. She told me that she would keep it together at work all day and then burst into tears in the car and cry all the way home. Her life became one long lament for her now former husband. "God," she prayed again and again, "bring him to the end of himself." Yet Debbie didn't make the lament central. She didn't demand that God bring Robert back. She did not give in to the power of her feelings. This is critical for the journey of love.

My father once told a young woman, a lingering hippie who had inhaled the spirit of our age, that she didn't have to act on her feelings. She said, "Really?" She had never heard that before. She'd always assumed that to be "true to yourself" meant you had to act on your feelings. The conversation was a moment of liberation for her. She realized that when we follow our feelings, we eventually become trapped by them. They define us. We think we can't love our spouse because we don't *feel* like we love him or her. We've defined love as a feeling over which we have no control. We are trapped.

Our modern age creates categories (grieving widow, terrible twos, bipolar) and then traps people in them. For instance, if we label two-year-olds with "terrible twos," then they are no longer responsible. So when they lose their tempers, they are just exhibiting the "terrible twos" instead of sin in need of discipline. Labeling returns us to the rigid world of paganism, which freezes everyone in a category: ethnic group, occupation, or social status. Widows do grieve, two-year-olds can be bad, but our behavior doesn't have to define us.

Naomi neither suppresses her feelings nor is trapped by them. So she determines to love her daughters-in-law no matter what it costs—even if it intensifies her anguish. That is *hesed*, pure and simple. But maybe you are saying, "I'm not sure I want to love like this." The only alternative is some form of self-love. And even that has a cost—it destroys your soul.

Hesed love is a determination to do someone good, no matter what, to be faithful to a covenant regardless of its impact on you. It wills to love when every fiber in your body screams *run*. This determination to love is at the heart of Jesus's relationship with his Father, and at the heart of ours as well. Not surprisingly, Jesus says: "If anyone would come after me, let him deny himself and take up his cross and follow me" (Mark 8:34). Paul the apostle says that this death of self united him with Jesus's death: "For we who are alive are always being given over to death for Jesus' sake, so that the life of Jesus also may be manifested in our mortal flesh. So death is at work in us, but life in you" (2 Cor. 4:11–12). That is the essence of Calvary love.

LOVE IS NOT GOD

Naomi has a problem. No matter how brilliant her logic, no matter how strong her will, no matter how deep her love—she can't shake Ruth. Ruth just won't go. Orpah did the sensible thing, but Ruth "clung to her" (Ruth 1:14). Naomi, not to be daunted, plays her last cards. She says, "See, your sister-in-law has gone back to her people and to her gods; return after your sister-in-law" (1:15).

Naomi appeals to peer pressure ("your sister-in-law has gone back") and to religious and cultural differences ("to her people and to her gods"). In other words, "Moab is your true home. Go where you're welcome, where you can find a husband." Her words reflect the view of ancient culture that hardwired gods, people, and land together.

Naomi is so caught up in selling her opinion that she goes pagan on us, encouraging Ruth to go back to the Moabite god Kemosh. Her words reflect the pagan culture of the book of Judges, where syncretism (combining faith in God with false gods) was rampant. As her lament was tinged with bitterness, so her faith is tinged with syncretism.

Don't Idolize Love

Naomi is focused on Ruth and her needs. That is good, but when we make the person we are loving (Ruth) the center of our life and not God, we are idolizing love. If love becomes the center, then Ruth's needs are more important than faithfulness to God. Compassion trumps truth. Naomi breaks the speed limit set by God's Word (no idols) by making love for Ruth the master goal.

Self-sacrificing love that isn't shaped by truth ends up as just another expression of human self-will. For example, Gandhi, seeking to embody

Jesus's command to love our enemies, urged the British to surrender to Hitler in the beginning of World War II.[1] Gandhi took a good principle (love) and separated it from truth (the evil of Hitler). In fact, the best way to love the Nazis was to go to war against them, to bring truth into their world. If love is not formed out of a dependence on God, out of Jesus's heart, which does nothing on its own (John 5:19), then love becomes off-centered or demanding. Naomi has become demanding, pushing Ruth toward what Naomi thinks is best for her.

Ruth, however, is immune to Naomi's final appeal. We can tell that Ruth has already made Yahweh and his people the center of her life because Naomi pleads with her to return with Orpah "to *her* people and *her* gods." Naomi has every reason to tell Ruth, "Go back to *your* people and *your* gods." It would make a better "sale," because it would join Ruth to Orpah, and it would remind Ruth that Moab is her true home. As a Moabite, Ruth is by definition in the ancient world a follower of Kemosh. But Naomi knows Ruth is a committed follower of Yahweh. So Ruth's response, which we'll consider next, is not a spur-of-the-moment, romantic promise, but a studied commitment to follow Yahweh. Ruth has done *hesed* with Yahweh before she does *hesed* with Naomi. That is how it works. Faith comes before love.

Ruth's Work of Art

Naomi is no pushover. She seals her appeal to Ruth with a command: "Return." This is Naomi's seventh command to Ruth in the space of just a few minutes, and the fourth time Naomi has told Ruth to "return."

Ruth first silences her mother-in-law with her own command, "Do not urge me to leave you or to return from following you." Then she pledges her love with an "incandescent reply that has set thirty centuries trembling":[2]

> For where you go I will go,
> and where you lodge I will lodge.
>
> Your people shall be my people,
> and your God my God.
>
> Where you die I will die,
> and there will I be buried.
> (Ruth 1:16–17, reformatted)

The artistry of the poem reflects Ruth's love. The first part of each line ("where you go") is matched by the second half ("I will go). Likewise, the first line of each stanza mirrors the second line. This pattern of doubling, called parallelism, is the primary structure of Hebrew poetry. Even today most good writing uses parallelism. John F. Kennedy's inaugural address is filled with parallelism, including the memorable, "Ask not what your country can do for you—ask what you can do for your country."

Ruth just as easily could have said to Naomi, "I'm not leaving you. I'm with you all the way." Instead, she creates a work of art, framing her act of love with beauty. Scholars describe her as a poet, but Ruth stands in a long tradition of women of faith who create works of art in poetry.[3]

God at the Center of Love

Each of the poem's three stanzas reflects Ruth's *hesed* love. In the first stanza Ruth commits to Naomi as a person, binding herself to Naomi for life. By pairing *going* and *lodging*, two activities that encompassed all of life, Ruth is committing to be with Naomi all the time.[4]

In the second stanza Ruth commits to Naomi's world, to her people and her God. One scholar reflects:

> "Your people will be my people, and your God my God" is a radical thought because it signals that Ruth is changing her identity in a world where that was almost inconceivable. The ancient world had no mechanism for religious conversion or change of citizenship; the very notion was unthinkable. Religion and peoplehood defined one's ethnic identity, and this could no more be changed than the color of one's skin.[5]

Ruth is not just going to be Naomi's servant; she embraces her whole life.

At first the third stanza seems superfluous, but in fact it transforms the first two. If Ruth had stopped after the first two stanzas, she could conceivably return to her people after Naomi dies. But in the third stanza Ruth commits to remaining in Bethlehem long after Naomi's death. Behind this third stanza is a deep understanding of the call of Israel's God. If Ruth returns to Moab and the worship of Kemosh after Naomi's death, then her commitment to Yahweh would be empty, shallow, just for the sake of human love. But Ruth puts God, not love, at the center of her love for Naomi. The form of her poem, with God at the center, mirrors the shape of her heart. She doesn't idolize love.

The disappointments we face in our quest for love are often formed by the quest itself. With public faith on the decline, people are hunting for new sources of life. What better form of life than love itself? That view leads to elevating love and marriage, thinking that finding the perfect mate will satisfy us. The Disney dream shapes how we approach marriage. So the perfect wedding is the new norm. Then when we realize we've married someone selfish, we discard the dream and become cynical about the possibility of love. We set ourselves up for failure by overloading love with far more than it can bear. Married love as a source of life crashes on the rocks of human depravity. The same happens with modern parenting. Parents want to be their kids' best friends. They want their children to have a pain-free world. The result is the child-centered home where children are a source of life. But love and relationships were never meant to be the center. Love is not god. God is love.

Implicit in Ruth's commitment to Yahweh is an understanding that God is not optional or secondary to life. He is all-consuming. The call of Yahweh is not from one tribal god to another, but the absolute call of the Creator God to see him as the true center of all things. The insignificant nation of Israel had the audacity to assert not only that (1) their God is more powerful than surrounding bigger nations, but also that (2) he is the Creator God of the whole earth, and, in fact, (3) the other gods don't even exist! When the Israelites lost a battle or were taken captive, they never considered that the other god beat up their God. They always saw God permitting the other nations to have victory because of their sin. They were unwavering in their audacity. It is but a small step from this mind-set to Jesus's absolute claim, "I am the way, and the truth, and the life" (John 14:6). There are no other options. There is no halfway option.

Ruth's commitment to Naomi foreshadows Jesus's call to his disciples to forsake all, including renouncing of family ties, for the sake of the kingdom (Matt. 10:37). Jesus's call perfectly matches his description of himself. If Jesus is the way, the truth, and the life, then his call transcends all other calls. It is absolute.

5

DEATH:
THE CENTER OF LOVE

Reflect for a minute on how we usually relate to people who are overwhelmed with a grief that won't go away. At worst we distance ourselves. At best we empathize with them or encourage them to go to counseling to work through their grief. Many professionals medicate them. None of that is inherently wrong, but none of that would help Naomi.

What she needs is lifelong physical help and companionship; she needs someone to die for her. She needs a savior. Ruth sees to the core of the issue and acts in her heart by binding herself to Naomi for life. Naomi has said, in effect, to Ruth and Orpah, "You have to save your life. In order to save your life, you have to lose me. My life is over." Ruth responds with, "No, my life is over."

A Small Picture of the Gospel
Figure 5.1 summarizes Ruth's love.

Figure 5.1. The gospel exchange of Ruth's love

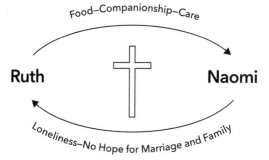

In order to give Naomi comfort, companionship, and food, Ruth
gives up friends, family, and the possibility of a husband and children—
in fact, her entire future. Ruth embraces hopelessness in order to give
Naomi a measure of hope. She out-*heseds* Naomi. Death is at the center
of Ruth's love.

What makes this so remarkable is that Ruth, too, is dealing with
the shock of widowhood. Embracing Naomi means embracing the stark
future of childlessness and namelessness that Naomi has painted for her.
One scholar puts it this way: "Ruth took on the uncertain future of a
bitter widow in a land where she knew no one, enjoyed few legal rights,
and—given the traditional Moabite-Israelite rivalry—faced possible ethnic prejudice. . . . She gave up a marriage to a man to devote herself to an
old woman—in a world dominated by men."[1]

Not surprisingly, some people are uncomfortable with the depth of
Ruth's love. One scholar cautions that Ruth's love not be used as a reason
for staying in abusive relationships.[2] I agree. If your husband hits you, call
the police. But it depends on what this scholar means by abuse. Many
close relationships have some low-level verbal abuse in them. It's what
sinners do to one another. A related concern: is Ruth enabling Naomi?
No, Ruth isn't supporting something bad; she's making good possible.
Naomi's on a good track; it's just a painful one.

In a culture dominated by the authoritative world of pop psychol-
ogy, we fear being trapped in a difficult relationship. Imagine a self-help
book with the title, *Seven Steps to Losing Your Life for Another Person*
or *Learn the Secret to Losing Power in Relationships*. But that is the essence of *hesed*. Love always narrows and limits our lives. It boxes us in.

Jill and I experience that every day with Kim. We've often gone for
three or more years without getting away alone because the combination
of finding a sitter and lack of funds was so challenging. Our favorite
date is running to McDonald's for an ice cream cone (only 150 calories
and $1.06!). But last time we did that, we lost electricity at home and
Kim panicked. So if you are feeling trapped, it could be because you are
engaged in *hesed* love.

Kim was our first teacher of *hesed* love. She helped transform us
because her needs were and are so demanding. We're continually forced
to stop and serve. That is, we settle down to watch a movie and Kim

walks in with a complaint or problem on her mind. With her autism we just can't tell Kim, "We'll deal with it later." We're getting used to being interrupted. Now she's God's gift to keep us from the old-age cranks!

God is trapped by his love for us.[3] God is bound to us in *hesed* love. Jeremiah 31:3 says,

> I have loved you with an everlasting love [*hesed*];
> therefore I have continued my faithfulness to you.

The person in the Old Testament who does *hesed* more than any other is God. In fact, God says, "I am *hesed*" (Jer. 3:12, my trans.). Despite Israel's rejection of him, God bound himself to his promises. The Father's binding commitment to Israel and to us leads to the gift of his Son. Jesus's *hesed* of us means that he turns his face to the cross and never looks back.

God does *hesed* to Naomi through Ruth. Ruth is God's answer to Naomi's lament.[4] Within seconds of Naomi's charge that "the hand of the Lord has gone out against me," Ruth's hands are clinging to Naomi in a fierce grip of love. Ruth is the face of God to Naomi. Our faces— how we reflect Christ in our gentleness, boldness, and love—are God's best picture of himself on earth. Ruth embodies the gospel. All acts of love done in faith are small pictures of the gospel. Our dying love replicates the dying love of Jesus.

Ruth's Victory

Ruth isn't finished. Like Naomi's speech, Ruth's builds slowly in emotional intensity to a powerful climax. She seals her multilayered commitment to Naomi with an oath: "May the Lord do so to me and more also if anything but death parts me from you" (Ruth 1:17). This is a classic Israelite oath where the actual "bad thing" that would happen to Ruth if she breaks the oath is left unstated. Instinctively we want to fill in the blank, "May the Lord do _____ to me and more so if . . ." Ruth pronounces a curse on herself if she fails to follow through with her *hesed*.

Naomi is stunned into silence. "And when Naomi saw that she was determined to go with her, she said no more" (1:18). You can't beat such a powerful love. It is almost overwhelming. The phrase "she was determined" in Hebrew means "she strengthened herself." Dying to self wasn't easy for Ruth. Like Naomi, Ruth put energy into her own death.

When I was explaining to a man I was discipling how death is the center of love, he recoiled from the thought. Then he laughed and said, "Loving my wife with a dying love is like asking me to drown myself in a bowl of water on the kitchen table." To put energy into the dying of self feels lousy. That is one of the many feelings of authentic love.

The Cost of Love

Naomi responds with silence. Ruth has just given up her life in an incredible act of selfless love, yet Naomi can't even muster a simple "thank you."

Love can be lonely. It does not remain so, but that is often where it does its best work. The greatest acts of love are almost always hidden. But, Jesus tells us, "There is nothing hidden that will not be disclosed" (Luke 8:17, NIV). As your face, your hands, and your heart begin to look like Jesus, people will notice him in you. They are always drawn to him. He is irresistible.

Why no "thank you"? We don't know, but suffering can narrow your life. The pain can be so intense that you become your pain. It doesn't have to, but pain can easily define you. Without realizing it, you can begin to see all of life through the lens of your pain. It can even be hard to accept love. You feel like a black hole, and you don't want people near you.

How does Ruth respond to Naomi's silence? She quietly walks with her to Bethlehem.[5] *Hesed* loves regardless of the response. It does not demand recognition or equality. It is uneven.

Consider this imaginary example of uneven love: A wife tries to develop intimacy with her husband through criticism. The theory behind her approach is that if he would get better, then she could love him. Let's say that the husband has been working at whatever his wife says. He uses her criticism as a way of making himself like Christ. And yet, the criticism keeps coming. It is almost a language, a way of relating. When he challenges his wife about whether she has a critical spirit, he just gets more criticism. The unfairness of love can wear on your soul. Over time the unevenness of love can get under our skin and a creeping bitterness can set in. Frankly, we can get tired of love. The husband is on the front lines of *hesed* love. How does he endure? How does Ruth endure?

The Power for Enduring Love

You endure the weight of love by being rooted in God. Your life energy needs to come from God, *not the person you are loving*. The more difficult the situation, the more you are forced into utter dependence on God. That is the crucible of love, where self-confidence and pride are stripped away, because you simply do not have the power or wisdom or ability in yourself to love. You know without a shadow of a doubt that you can't love. That is the beginning of faith—knowing you can't love.

Faith is the power for love. Paul the apostle tells us that the I beam or hidden structure of the Christian life is "faith working through love" (Gal. 5:6). Faith energizes love. We handle the weight of love by rooting ourselves in God. Our inability to sustain love drives us into dependence on God. Then faith becomes a continuous cry. Like the tax collector in the temple, we cry out, "God, be merciful to me, a sinner!" (Luke 18:13).

In overwhelming situations where you are all out of human love, you discover that you are praying all the time because you can't get from one moment to the next without God's help. You realize you can't do life on your own, and you need God and his love to be the center. You lean upon God because you can't bear the weight of love. So faith is not a mountain to climb, but a valley to fall into.

How do we know this is happening in Ruth? First, Ruth says she is resting the weight of her life on God: "Your God will be my God." Second, Boaz will later tell Ruth that she has taken shelter "under the wings of God" (Ruth 2:12). Finally, compare Abraham's faith with Ruth's, as many scholars have done because the book of Ruth is filled with allusions to Genesis.[6] In Genesis 12:1–3, Abraham, like Ruth, steps out in faith to leave his home and come to the Promised Land. But the similarities end there. One scholar puts it this way:

> Ruth stands alone; she possesses nothing. No God has called her; no deity has promised her blessing; no human being has come to her aid. She lives and chooses without a support group, and she knows that the fruit of her decision may well be the emptiness of rejection, indeed of death. Consequently, not even Abraham's leap of faith surpasses this decision of Ruth's. And there is

more. Not only has Ruth broken with family, country, and faith, but she has also reversed sexual allegiance. A young woman has committed herself to the life of an old woman rather than to the search for a husband. . . . One female has chosen another female in a world where life depends upon men. There is no more radical decision in all the memories of Israel.[7]

We are at ground zero of a biblical explosion of faith. So we wonder, if God took Abraham's faith and made him a father of many nations, what might God do with Ruth's faith?

Ruth the Lover

We come alive as we love. The depth and quality of Ruth's character emerge when she binds herself in love. She's an unusual combination of quiet power and love, intimidated neither by Naomi nor by the prospect of suffering. In fact, she fights to embrace suffering. She will not be out-loved. And she is thoughtful, actually brilliant. Her offer of herself as a living sacrifice is the only answer to Naomi's pain.

Call it boldness, courage, or daring; Ruth goes right after life. She does not waver in her response to Naomi. In fact, she is so powerful that she leaves the ever-articulate Naomi speechless. And she's an artist. The beauty of her love matches the beauty of her poetic response. Ruth sparkles when she loves.

As we love "in place," as we love the people that God has permitted in our world, the texture of Jesus emerges in us. Our beauty comes not from pursuing a brilliant career track, but in the nitty-gritty endurance with difficult people or circumstances.

6

ENTERING A
BROKEN HEART

The two widows, dressed in black mourning garb, make their way north down to the Jordan Valley, then west past Jericho, up the steep escarpment along the desert path to the Judean highlands, and finally south to Bethlehem: "So the two of them went on until they came to Bethlehem. And when they came to Bethlehem, the whole town was stirred because of them. And the women said, 'Is this Naomi?'" (Ruth 1:19).

A better translation for the Hebrew word for *stirred* is "echoed with excitement." The town is abuzz. They haven't seen Naomi in ten years. Questions tumble out. Is this Naomi? Where are her husband and sons? Who is this strange woman with her?

A midsized city like Bethlehem would have only one main gate, so Naomi cannot slip in through a side gate unnoticed. The gate was in the shape of a corridor flanked by chambers on both sides (fig. 6.1). Everything happened here. It combined Walmart, the Internet, and city hall.

Figure 6.1. Typical Israelite city gate[1]

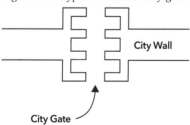

When we've been away from home for ten years and out of touch, we typically come up to people, catch their eyes, and if we sense they don't recognize us, we say, "Hi, Susie, it's me!" But Naomi doesn't say a word. There is no "It's me" or "So good to see you again." We know this because the women aren't sure they recognize her. They ask each other, "Is this Naomi?" The years and grief have likely taken their toll on Naomi, causing the women to hesitate when she doesn't identify herself. Naomi's entrance fits with her struggle. It's easy to get lost in our pain, particularly with close family and friends.

As Naomi enters the city, exhausted from the long climb through the desert and weary of soul, she remembers she left these same gates with a husband and two sons. She sees the furtive glances from familiar faces and the hushed question, "Is this *Pleasant*?" passing from woman to woman.[2] The disparity between the meaning of her name and the reality of her life cuts her soul like a knife. Her life is anything but pleasant. Her heart spills over in a spontaneous lament, and she cries out:

> Do not call me Naomi; call me Mara,
>> for the Almighty has dealt very bitterly with me.
>> I went away full, and the Lord has brought me back empty.
> Why call me Naomi,
>> when the Lord has testified against me
>> and the Almighty has brought calamity upon me? (1:20–21,
>>> reformatted)

Naomi is saying, "Beautiful? Nothing could be further from the truth. I am bitter (Mara), and the mighty One has made me that way."

Considering that these are her first words to friends she hasn't seen in years, Naomi's tone seems blunt, almost explosive. Why that tone? Because we tend to let it all hang out with people who are close to us. It is safer to be ourselves. Plus celebration hurts when we suffer. The town wants a party; Naomi wants to disappear.

Understanding Naomi's Lament

We can better understand Naomi's lament by looking at the patterns of poetry. Notice how the repetition of her name and the word "call" in lines 1 and 4 divide the poem into two stanzas. Then within the stanzas she creates an artistic flourish by inverting the two names for God ("the Almighty" and "the LORD").[3]

In each stanza Naomi uses a different picture to convey her grief. In the first she compares herself to a clay jar; she left full and came back empty. In the second she uses the image of the law court, saying, "Yahweh has testified against me." Not only is the Almighty her Judge, but he also witnesses against her. What recourse does she have when the court is stacked against her?

How do we sort this out? First, Naomi is being real, authentic. If she puts on a spiritual mask with God, she will be a hypocrite. God would no longer be accessible because the real Naomi would no longer be encountering the real God. Second, her faith in God drives her frustration with God. Because she believes that he is both good and powerful, she is in agony.

Naomi lives in the tension between hope and reality. That is, she faces the reality of her circumstances while simultaneously longing for them to be different. She doesn't collapse the tension but lives in the murky middle. That is faith at its simplest. The result? Her heart breaks. Our modern age removes the tension by dropping either God's goodness or his power and then drifts into cynicism. It resigns prematurely to the brokenness of life. It gives up. Figure 6.2 captures Naomi's agony. As a daughter of Yahweh believing in the promises of God, she hopes, but her life is hopeless. The gap between hope and reality is the desert. Naomi's lament is the prayer of the desert, the agony of living in the tension between hope and reality.

Figure 6.2. The desert: hope versus reality

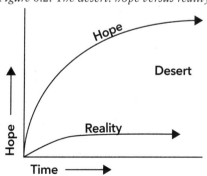

No one in the story criticizes Naomi for being disrespectful of God—not the narrator, nor the village women, nor Ruth. Nor does God. He just quietly wraps her in his arms for the rest of her life.

Love Listens to Laments

The church has not been particularly good at hearing laments from its broken people. Personally, I don't like listening to laments. They are disorderly, unnerving. I like things tidy. Laments break the pattern of seemingly appropriate politeness to God. They feel out of balance.

When Jill and I were first married (we were eighteen and nineteen), she realized within six months that something was wrong with me. She wasn't sure I was a Christian. Neither was I. I remember her lying in bed pouring her heart out in a desperate prayer for me. I hated her prayer. I recoiled from her outpouring of passion. Two years later God quietly changed my heart. God heard Jill's lament.

Jill responded to my poverty of spirit with her own poverty of spirit. That's what a lament does. That's why I recoiled from it. The very thing I needed, poverty of spirit, was the shape of Jill's lament. A lament puts us in an openly dependent position, where our brokenness reflects the brokenness of the world. It's pure authenticity. Holding it in, not giving voice to the lament, can be a way of putting a good face on it. But to not lament puts God at arm's length and has the potential of splitting us. We appear okay, but we are really brokenhearted.

A lament functions like a mirror of the world. What is broken or out of balance is not the lament but the world. Motivated by clear seeing, a lament reacts to the mismatch between hope and reality, between heaven and earth.

A friend went to the funeral of a lesbian relative. The funeral presented a moving postmodern montage that included Handel's *Messiah* and Buddhist poetry. My friend found herself being captured by the gentle spirit of the presenters. I encouraged her to be broken by it, to lament over the seduction of beauty and the cherry-picking of Christian hope. Outside of Jesus, dead is dead. Because we believe in the goodness of God, we are broken by its absence.

A broken heart that doesn't lament can breed unbelief. A friend of mine was leading a missions trip to Europe and was struck by how many nonbelievers were going to pubs. That was their church. It seemed impossible to reach them. His spirit was overwhelmed by the power of the culture. I urged him instead to let his heart be broken over it.

Listening to a lament is a powerful way of loving someone who is suffering. By being present, by not correcting or even offering our own unique brand of Christian encouragement ("It's going to be all right— God's in control"), we give those who are grieving space to be themselves.

That doesn't mean that Naomi's judgment of God is correct. God is good and just. He will answer her frustration with more goodness. Naomi was interpreting God through the lens of her experience. She stopped in the middle of the story and measured God. A deeper faith waits until the end of the story and interprets experience through the lens of God's faithfulness. Is this something we tell Naomi? No. It is what we tell ourselves. Good theology lets us endure quietly with someone else's pain when all the pieces aren't together. It acts like invisible faith-glue.

A lament fits God's heart perfectly. God loves an open, honest heart, no matter how broken by life, even if theologically incorrect. How else could Jesus invite everyone who was weary and heavy laden to come to him for rest? He invites us to come as we are—all messed up—with our grief and our emotions. God not only did not condemn Moses's and Elijah's laments, but recorded them as part of Scripture (Ex. 5:22; 1 Kings 17:20).

Entering Naomi's Grief

When we hear a lament, we enter into that person's pain. That's called incarnation, and it is the most basic structure of love. That is what Ruth does with Naomi. She enters Naomi's world and lets the weight of that world come on her. To enter a broken heart means that our hearts will be broken as well. That's what happened to Jesus. That's the gospel.

Let us try to enter Naomi's grief. Not only is she without hope, but her very existence pains her beyond belief. When the sun comes up in the morning, it feels strange. She stumbles along in a daze, unsure of where she is. Nor does she care. She hears people and sees them, but they are like shadows. For all practical purposes, she has died.

Paul the apostle described this state: "For we were so utterly burdened beyond our strength that we despaired of life itself. Indeed, we felt that we had received the sentence of death" (2 Cor. 1:8–9). The suffering is so strong, so multilayered, that you lose your bearings. You are enveloped by it. You have become your pain.

Deep soul grief isolates you. Even your friends pull back confused, unsure of how to handle you. To enter your pain feels like they are entering a bottomless black hole where they too will lose their bearings. It is safer to stay outside. At Gethsemane the disciples were "sleeping for sorrow"—withdrawing from Jesus's pain because it was so overwhelming (Luke 22:45).

Many years ago when our daughter Kim was born with multiple disabilities, some of my wife's friends found her grief overwhelming and pulled back. It was too hard to bear with someone whose problems didn't go away quickly. We've not been taught that to love someone means we enter their suffering. We don't realize that the normal Christian life is to "share [Jesus's] sufferings, becoming like him in his death" (Phil. 3:10). So when faced with a problem that wouldn't go away (Kim) and a raw broken heart (Jill), some pulled away.

Protecting Yourself from Bitterness

The opposite danger of not lamenting is over-lamenting. Dwelling on a lament is the breeding ground for bitterness. Bitterness is a wound nursed. Our culture's emphasis on the sacredness of feelings often gives people an unspoken theology of bitterness. They feel entitled to it.

Bitterness can be subtle. It leaks out as gossip, a joyless spirit, or just the quiet revenge of withdrawing your spirit from someone. When listening to a friend, I noticed he'd pulled back from a Christian brother ever so slightly, so I probed, asking him if he was struggling with low-level bitterness. He said no, but a week later he thanked me. The expression "low-level" had pricked his conscience. He was used to thinking of bitterness in neon lights, not realizing that most bitterness is just a soft, quiet killer, a creeping soul death.

Is Naomi bitter? Several things suggest she is on a slippery slope. She silently enters the city without introducing herself, snaps at the women's joyous welcome, telling them to call her "bitter," and ignores Ruth. And finally, her lament is not a prayer directed toward God but an accusation about him. Her God is sovereign, but her theology is "sovereignty without grace."[4] How do we keep our lament from drifting into bitterness? Hebrew scholar Tremper Longman reflects:

> There are many examples from the Psalms where there is a healthy raising of the fist to God. There are also examples of unhealthy raising of the fist, notably the wilderness. The difference is that in the healthy they are speaking to God, not to others. Because they are praying to God as they accuse him, there is a sense of hope. So is Naomi like the psalmist or like the Israelites in the wilderness?[5]

Unlike the Israelites who wanted to return to Egypt, Naomi is obeying, doing the right thing by returning to the Promised Land. Her feelings were all over the place, but she put one foot in front of the other as she returned. We can summarize her response this way:

Bitterness openly expressed to God + obedience ⇨ a raw, pure form of faith

Bitterness openly expressed + disobedience ⇨ rebellion

Through a sheer act of the will, Naomi continues to show up for life. In C. S. Lewis's *Screwtape Letters*, the senior devil, Screwtape, warns his junior devil of the danger of this obedience:

> Do not be deceived, Wormwood. Our cause [the Devil's cause] is never more in danger than when a human, no longer desiring, but still intending to do our Enemy's will [God's will], looks round upon a universe from which every trace of Him seems to have vanished, and asks why he has been forsaken, and still obeys.[6]

Naomi's obedience in the face of suffering and disappointment is the essence of faith.

DISCOVERING GLORY
IN LOVE

After all the emotional intensity of the opening scenes, now the curtain closes quietly on the first chapter of Ruth: "So Naomi returned, and Ruth the Moabite her daughter-in-law with her, who returned from the country of Moab. And they came to Bethlehem at the beginning of barley harvest" (Ruth 1:22).

The narrator subtly reminds us that Naomi forgets something, namely, Ruth. When Naomi says, "I've come back empty" (1:21), Ruth is standing right beside her. As Naomi lets out her anguished accusations of God, he too is silently present. As she walks into the city, bitter and angry, in the midst of her enemies of death and despair, God has set a table before her. God says nothing in the face of Naomi's raw challenge. He just loves.

Ruth's silence suggests that she accepts the ambiguity that is Naomi. Ruth loves Naomi as she is, not as she wants her to be. That is an important move on the journey of love. Scripture presents people not as cardboard cutouts, but as richly textured men and women who are seldom neat packages of good or evil, but often "an abiding mystery," "a bundle of paradoxes."[1] We often get stuck on the dark side of a person. We fixate on the depravity. One of the worst effects of our fallen natures is that we read everything as fallen. We over-read evil and, frankly, become judgmental. Love accepts the paradox.

By mentioning Moab twice, the narrator emphasizes Ruth's vulnerability. She is a stranger in a strange land. Naomi seems to have forgotten that Ruth is also suffering, a childless widow for whom marriage is a lost dream. Why doesn't Naomi see Ruth? As we've seen, suffering can narrow our vision. That makes Jesus's Passion all the more remarkable. When Jesus is under tremendous pressure, he never stops loving. When the women weep over him as he walks to Golgotha, Jesus is more concerned for their coming suffering than for his own. Remember, observations such as "suffering narrows our vision" are not rules. We are not trapped by descriptions of life. The person of Jesus defines life for us, allowing us not to be locked in by our circumstances. The Spirit of Jesus gives us the power to love, no matter what our circumstances.

What does that mean for us? Even in overwhelming, difficult situations, we don't have to be controlled by our feelings. Like Naomi, we can express our feelings, but we can still do the right thing.

Bearing the Cost of Love

Ruth's walk through the city gates, ignored and unthanked, vividly portrays the cost of love. Ruth bears the weight of Naomi's life. We usually recoil from the cost of love, thinking it is an alien substance, but it is the essence of love. This is strangely encouraging because when the pressure of love builds, we think that somehow we showed up for the wrong life. This isn't what we signed up for. But no, this is the divine path called love.

I was encouraging a friend of mine, Leslie, with this insight of the cost of love. She was rejected by her family because she patiently endured with her wayward husband. Her eyes filled with tears as I told her that it was okay to bear the cost of her husband's sin. (The husband had shown genuine repentance.) Instead of being angry at her family, she allowed their rejection of her to draw her into the dying of Jesus, into Christ. Paul describes this kind of love when he says, "For we who live are always being given over to death for Jesus' sake, so that the life of Jesus may also be manifested in our mortal flesh" (2 Cor. 4:11).

Knowing the shape of one-way love gave Leslie the persistence to continue to pursue her family in love, even though they continued to reject her. Why was this knowledge so helpful? It reframes the conflict from merely a human or horizontal dimension to a divine or vertical one. Instead of you against me, your sin against me draws me into Christ. Leslie wasn't pretending that her husband didn't have a sinful past. She was bearing the weight of his past. *Hesed* love doesn't pretend everything is rosy. In fact, because it knows things aren't rosy, it sets its will to love *regardless of the response of the one loved.*

I've watched another friend of mine, Peter, bear the cost of *hesed.* Some twenty years ago his wife had a breakdown and slipped into mild schizophrenia. Recently she got an inheritance, left Peter, and moved out of state to Michigan. About every six weeks he drives out to Michigan to be with her for a long weekend, to fix up the house. She's thankful to see him, but has told him recently that she no longer considers them married and has hinted at an affair. She constantly criticizes him, and her shifting moods leave my friend often wondering how to love her. I've told Peter that biblically he does not have to remain married, but he hesitates. He told me, "When I said 'for better or for worse' that included mental illness and meanness. I've got to play out the hand that the Lord has given me." As Peter has endured with his wayward wife, it has softened him. Loving a difficult woman has gentled my friend.

Finding Strength for the Hidden Work of Love

When we care for a hurting person or live with a difficult spouse, that person often doesn't have a lot of love to give us. Important but peripheral truths like "communication skills" and "the need to confront" just don't cut it. They lack the power to sustain us in the hidden work of love. When we confront a self-righteous person, we just get more criticism. When we try to communicate with a narcissist, he or she will dominate the conversation. Over time this can wear on our spirit. Only the core passions of Christianity—love and faith—can sustain us in the hidden work of love.

Once when I was bearing the cost of betrayal, I found myself withdrawing emotionally. It felt like I was suffocating. To keep my heart from drifting, I clung to Scripture and for several years prayed daily for grace to bear the cost. As I prayed, God remapped my soul. Here are some of the Scriptures I prayed:

> Be completely humble and gentle; be patient, bearing with one another in love. (Eph. 4:2, NIV)

> Bear with each other and forgive whatever grievances you may have against one another. Forgive as the Lord forgave you. (Col. 3:13, NIV)

> Above all, love each other deeply, because love covers a multitude of sins. (1 Pet. 4:8, NIV)

I remember feeling almost hungry for these words. I had to learn a new way to live, to think. These words burned themselves on my heart. When that happens, the hidden work of love opens the door to glory.

Ruth's Hidden Glory

Ruth walks into the city ignored and, in effect, alone. One of the hardest parts of a *hesed* love is that you can love others, but there may be no one to love you. The very act of loving can make you lonely. At the cross the religious leaders hurled this fear at Jesus: "He saved others; he cannot save himself" (Matt. 27:42). They were correct. George Orwell wrote, "One is prepared in the end to be defeated and broken up by life, which is the inevitable price of fastening one's love upon other human individuals."[2]

But that loneliness, that dying, instead of being the end of you, can display Jesus's beauty in you. The moment when you think everything has gone wrong is exactly the moment when the beauty of God is shining through you. True glory is almost always hidden—when you are enduring quietly with no cheering crowd. When old soldiers gather to reflect on their wartime experience, they don't think of the medal ceremony when the world honors their valor. They think of the battle, the sacrifice, and the endurance—that is their glory. When for the thousandth time you quietly forgive someone who will never know your pain, that is your glory. When you continually do a household chore unthanked and maybe even criticized, that is your glory. Hidden love shreds the ego. Walking into Bethlehem alone, a foreigner, without a male protector—with only Yahweh—that is Ruth's glory.

Ruth's greatest Son will take a similar walk, utterly alone in an act of supreme love. That too will be his hour of glory. John highlights three times that the cross was Jesus's hour of glory (John 12:23; 13:31; 17:1). John Stott puts it this way: "What is striking about John's presentation is that . . . [Jesus's] glory . . . was above all to be seen in his present weakness, in the self-humiliation of his incarnation."[3] Your moment of glory is when you are seen for who you really are, when the best of you is on parade. According to Paul, our shame is God's vessel for glory (1 Cor. 4:9). Ruth's quiet, lonely love shows us all the best in her.

I saw the glory of enduring love in a friend of mine, Tom. He had gone to his boss, a pastor, about how this man was treating other staff. His boss was not used to being confronted, so Tom's concerns felt odd, out of place. In response, his boss quietly marginalized him. Tom wasn't invited to key meetings. His name disappeared from reports. At leadership meetings, the pastor would occasionally belittle him. When this happened, Tom usually froze on the inside, completely powerless. Then Tom remembered that Jesus said his life was like a seed that dies. "The hour has come for the Son of Man to be glorified. Truly, truly, I say to you, unless a grain of wheat falls into the earth and dies, it remains alone; but if it dies, it bears much fruit" (John 12:23–24).

Tom realized that he was in a glory moment. By accepting the shame that God had permitted in his life, by going through this living death, he was displaying God. It was Tom's glory. The dying was up to Tom; the resurrection was up to God. So Tom became a professional at dying! He says he still remembers that moment: shamed on the outside, but glowing on the inside. God used that dying to repeatedly humble Tom and shape him like Christ. I've been watching Tom's life for twenty years now since that dying began, and God has done nothing but bring resurrection.

God's grace works most powerfully when there is no exit, when we learn to love because we have no other choice. We experience a strange and powerful presence of God during those moments of hidden love. When you hang in there on the journey of love, when you endure and don't take the exits of distance and cynicism, God shows up. Contra Orwell, "broken up by life" is the place where we get to know God. His presence is a down payment on the coming resurrection. It is so strong that you can almost touch him. Because of the Father's presence through the Spirit of Jesus, we are not alone on the journey of love. Jesus refers to this when hours before his own death he tells his disciples, "If anyone loves me, he will keep my word, and my Father will love him, and we will come to him and make our home with him" (John 14:23). Jesus is the only person who was alone as he loved. We are a resurrection people, and that makes all the difference.

8

LOVING AGAINST
MY FEELINGS

Notice how the narrator emphasizes the word "returned" in the closing summary: "So Naomi returned, and Ruth the Moabite her daughter-in-law with her, who returned from the country of Moab" (Ruth 1:22).

In Hebrew the word translated "return" (*shub*) can mean repent. The repeated use of the word "return" (twelve times in chap. 1)[1] suggests a kind of repentance on Naomi's part. Elimelech's family left the Promised Land for a heathen nation. Evidently most other Bethlehemites did not leave. And in Moab, the sons married non-Israelites.[2] One scholar writes, "Like Abraham's excursion to Egypt in Gen. 12:10–20, the family's move to Moab to escape the famine looks like a lapse of spiritual commitment."[3] Leaving gardens, like Eden and Canaan, is never a good idea.

Another hint that Elimelech's family may have been unwise to leave Israel is how the narrator describes the family's changing intentions in their move to Moab. In Ruth 1:1 they plan to "sojourn" for a brief stay. But in verse 2 they "remained there" and, finally, in verse 4 they "lived there about ten years." The alert Israelite reader would have recognized the same pattern in Lot's slow descent into Sodom.[4]

Repentance often drives the journey of love. It moves the story forward. Because Naomi returned home, God's grace will be unleashed in her life. Repentance involves a returning to the box, to the world of limits, that my Father has given me. I stop creating my own story and submit to the story that God is weaving. For example, before G. K. Chesterton became a believer, he realized that life had a fairy-tale structure to it.[5] In a fairy tale, a limitless opportunity (Cinderella at the ball) has a limiting factor (be home by midnight). Naomi has decided to come home by midnight.

Life is like a beautiful garden with a tree whose fruit I can't touch. That "no" defines and shapes my life in the garden. So my relationship with my wife is like a wonderful garden with a solitary "no": I cannot touch or develop emotional intimacy with another woman. That "no" narrows and limits my life. It provides a frame for my love to Jill. I am keenly aware that I can destroy a forty-year marriage in five minutes. That limiting, instead of boxing us in, lets the story come alive.

Repentance as Gentle Rain

We're always leaving the box. At a difficult time in my life when multiple relationships had imploded, God continually brought Isaiah 30:15 to mind: "In repentance and rest is your salvation" (NIV). I wanted other people to repent. God wanted me to repent. I sensed God closing all the doors in my life except the one marked "Repentance." So I dismissed thoughts of justice ("I'm being unfairly treated") and put my energy into repentance. I pursued even those who had wronged me and asked them, "What have I done wrong?" I shifted my energy from solving the problem to hunting for my sin.

As part of that shift, I began to pray daily that I would love, even prize, correction. Getting rebuked, especially if I thought it was unjust, was not one of my favorite activities. So I wrote up several prayer cards from Proverbs, all with the focus that "a wise man listens to rebukes." Years later, I still live in the aura of that humbling. It affects how I lead meetings, like one I had recently.

In a staff meeting I was sharing my concern that mysticism influences how some evangelicals think about prayer. I read an example of what I was talking about and noticed that one staff member's face went flat. I paused the meeting and asked her if something was bothering her. She said, "I agree with what you said, but I'm concerned that you are communicating that our ministry is special, unique." I was immediately convicted. The way I had read that example lacked humility. I thanked her for her honesty. The check in her spirit protected our work from my pride. Like Naomi, I came home. Home for me is the low-place where I'm not special, where I'm simply faithful to the calling that God has given me.

Repentance can be dramatic, but most repentance is a gentle rain, slowly softening the hardened soil of our hearts. Repentance can be just seeing yourself or someone else in a new way. If we focus just on big repentances, we can unwittingly become demanding, insisting that people absorb more change than they can make all at once. Seeing repentance as a gentle rain can make our rebukes gentler. Instead of going for a home run, we can go for singles. We can be thankful for small turns of the soul. In Psalm 23, the Lord "restores my soul" (v. 3). The Hebrew word for "restores" is *shub*, which means "turn" or "return." When Naomi returns to Israel, to the house of the Lord, her own soul is restored.

Repentance is not merely conviction. It does something: Naomi returns. She returns complaining, depressed, angry, and withdrawn. But she returns. What a visual of Jesus's invitation to all "those who are weary and heavy laden." Weary and heavy laden people are not always pleasant. C. S. Lewis says that he came to faith "kicking, struggling, resentful, and darting his eyes in every direction for a chance to escape."[6] Because of our fallen nature, we often repent badly. But that's Jesus's point. We don't get cleaned up before we come to him; we come messy, grumpy, with a self-centered heart. But it is important to come! Paul tells us that "God's kindness is meant to lead you to repentance" (Rom. 2:4).

In my experience, people apologize badly. If you speak an honest word to them, they rarely say, "Oh, thank you for that rebuke. I've felt pride welling up in my heart all morning. Your honesty has restored my soul." More typically I hear, "I know I am wrong, but you do the same thing," or just a flat, passionless, "I'm sorry," which can mean, "I'm apologizing because I got caught." Or they retaliate or withdraw emotionally. But if I'm doing *hesed* love, if I've accepted that life is uneven, then, like God, I can accept even a grumpy apology. The humility that characterizes *hesed* love absorbs the other person's pride like a giant sponge and keeps me from turning the apology into a quarrel.

The Dislocation of Authentic Love

Naomi repents by obediently returning to her homeland, even though it feels awful. Ruth obediently stays with Naomi, even though Ruth, as we'll see later, is scared and lonely. They both feel dislocated because of the mismatch between their emotions (anguish) and their wills (doing the right thing). It is particularly painful for Naomi because she is returning to her God who appears to be against her. So the very act of obedience makes her feel dislocated, out of place.

Because our culture makes feeling happy the goal, when our feelings are negative, when we experience the cost of love, we think that something has gone wrong, that we're not being true to ourselves. Remember Robert who left his wife Debbie, telling her, "I don't have any feelings for you anymore"? He went on to cloak his self-centeredness in the language of integrity. He told Debbie: "I need to be honest with myself. I'm no longer in love with you. I was doing everything for duty and obligation, and now it's time to think about me, time for me to live my life the way I want to live it. I've fallen in love with someone I met online." He used "authenticity" to cover his betrayal. As a result Debbie was not only abandoned and betrayed, but also guilty and confused.

Our "in tune with my feelings" era believes that to be true to myself, to be authentic, means I need to act on my feelings. But the opposite is true. In fact, true authenticity means I maintain a trust through thick and thin. To obey when I don't feel like it means I will feel dislocated. That frees me because it allows me to do good no matter what my internal spirit is doing. When that happens, I am on my way to maturity, to becoming a seasoned pilgrim of love.

The modern quest for authenticity has become twisted into a quest to have our will and our emotions in sync. This faux authenticity is just a fancy version of the sixties slogan, "If it feels good, do it." So the celebration of being "true to yourself" means acting on your feelings. "I'm not in love with my spouse anymore, so I'm going to leave." This oft-repeated formula, the logic behind many broken covenants, equates love with feeling happy. The result? We are dominated by the tyranny of our ever-changing feelings. We don't endure.

Almost every ancient culture knew that unchecked feelings were dangerous. Even the Greek Stoics knew that if you followed your desires you were headed for disaster. Our culture has created an idol out of feelings and become enslaved to them. We have become emotional chameleons, captive to our mercurial desires. "Being happy all the time, pretending to be happy, actually attempting to be happy—it's exhausting," writes novelist Stephen Marche in *The Atlantic*. Marche quotes a study on happiness: "Valuing happiness is not necessarily linked to greater happiness."[7]

True authenticity, when I'm obeying in spite of my emotions, always makes me feel dislocated. My feelings say "drop out," but my commitment says "hang in there." If I hang in there, eventually my feelings will right themselves and will catch up with my obedience. We'll see that happen in Naomi's life.

On the other hand, if I am ruled by the desire to feel happy, I become split, divided. Refusing to love with dislocated feelings leads to a divided soul. Dislocated feelings are the temporary cost inherent in love, but a divided soul destroys me. Ironically, the modern quest for wholeness invariably leads to this splintering of the self. That's what happened to Robert.

After Robert left Debbie, he moved in with another woman. But he wanted to continue to have a friendly relationship with Debbie, to take her out to lunch occasionally. He also wanted to be close to his grandkids. He missed the emotional intimacy with his wife, but at the same time he wanted to be sexually intimate with another woman. In other words, he wanted to separate his life into distinct categories—thus dividing himself. He was inauthentic. Fortunately for Robert, his wife refused to offer him emotional support, and his daughter refused to give him unfettered access to the grandkids. Robert wanted life on his own terms; his family offered him wholeness and integrity. It opened a door in Robert's heart to repentance.

Ruth gives us a perfect example of authenticity. Her deeds match her words. She commits to *hesed*, then does *hesed*. Her will (what she does) is shaped by her *hesed*, her passions (her love for God and Naomi). So her path or trajectory goes something like this:

Ruth's *hesed* of Naomi (words) ⇨ Ruth's enduring in love with Naomi (deeds)

Ruth obeys by following through. She does what she told Naomi she would do. Naomi obeys by returning to the Land of Promise. For both the obedience feels nasty. They both feel dislocated, out of sync with their feelings. In a fallen world this dislocation is one of the primary feelings of love. That is why endurance is the heartbeat of *hesed* love. And the nature of endurance is hanging in there in opposition to your feelings.

The question is not "How do I feel about this relationship?" but "Have I been faithful to my word, to the covenants I am in?" As Jesus says in the Sermon on the Mount, "If you love those who love you, what reward do you have? Do not even the tax collectors do the same?" (Matt. 5:46). In other words, if I love only when I feel like it, then I've really not understood love. *Hesed* love loves in opposition to our feelings. Love like this strips us of self-will and purifies our motivations. It is surprisingly liberating because we're not trapped by either our feelings or the other person's response. When neither preserving the relationship nor our feelings are central, we're free to offer the other person a rich tapestry of love.

Part Two

THE SHAPE OF
THE JOURNEY

THE GOSPEL SHAPE
OF LOVE

Hope is the faint glimmer on the distant horizon. It keeps you moving on the journey of love. The closing scene of the first chapter of Ruth ends with a hint of hope: "And they came to Bethlehem at the beginning of the barley harvest" (Ruth 1:22).

The spring harvest was a joyous time. Food! Beer! (That's what they made from barley.)[1] The barley harvest began in late April, and according to the Gezer calendar, was one month long and was followed by the month-long wheat harvest culminating in the Feast of Pentecost.[2]

The phrase "they came" also suggests hope. The tense of the verb connotes good fortune, as if to say, "now it happened that they came . . ." But the Hebrews did not believe in chance; they believed that Yahweh ordered the universe.[3] Because Yahweh controlled even chance, they were willing to cast lots to make important decisions. "Now it happened" is a veiled reference to God's unseen orchestration. And Ruth and Naomi *just happened* to come at the *beginning*!

The hints of hope continue as the narrator introduces Boaz: "Now Naomi had a relative of her husband's, a worthy man of the clan of Elimelech, whose name was Boaz" (2:1). "Worthy man" is a two-word phrase in Hebrew: *gibbor hayil. Gibbor* is a "great man," often meaning "warrior." *Hayil* means "worthy or excellent." In short, Boaz was a powerful, dignified, good man. Every large community has powerful men, but not all of them are good. *Boaz* means "in him [*bo*] is strength [*az*]." So we wonder why the narrator tells us about him. Are we going to meet this man again?

The story started with a relentless downward motion into despair, but now it begins to turn upward. Famine and departure are being replaced by harvest and return. Ruth's love and vitality are countering Naomi's dark, downward spiral. Resurrection is in the air. But resurrection was foreign to the ancient world.

The Pagan View: Trapped in the Circle of Life

Every ancient civilization—from the Cherokee Indians in North America to Taoist monks in China—believed that life is circular. As they looked out at the horizon they saw a circle. Every day was a time circle, beginning with morning and ending with night. The moon traced a circle of light during the course of a month. The sun had an annual circle following the seasons. Every life was a circle beginning with birth and ending with death (fig. 9.1). The circle is the symbol for paganism. So by definition, nothing new happened in ancient paganism.

Figure 9.1. Circle of life and death

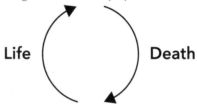

But it wasn't a happy circle. The Greeks believed we are caught in this cycle. For example, Homer's *Iliad* begins with Odysseus leaving home and the *Odyssey* ends with Odysseus returning home—he goes full circle. But it is a cycle of despair: empires rise to glory and fall to ashes. A serious Greek play always ends in tragedy. Why? Because even in the best of times, suffering waits just around the corner, haunting every celebration.[4] Heraclitus, living in Ephesus five hundred years before Jesus, wrote:

> As all things change to fire,
> and fire exhausted
> falls back into things . . . .
> The way up is the way back.
> The beginning is the end.[5]

Thomas Cahill observes:

> The message of the Sibyl [a Greek prophetic "spirit"] . . . seems to have been that, though some times are better and some worse, there can be no permanent safety. Peace will be followed by war, prosperity by poverty, happiness by suffering, life by death. This was indeed the constant message of all ancient literature and its principal insight into human existence.[6]

Our modern world, having rejected the way of the cross, tries to find a new center to life by combining ancient paganism with secularized Christian optimism. We see this romanticism in the Disney *Lion King*'s rejoicing in the circle of life. But paganism isn't optimistic. It knows that the celebration of the circle is naïve. What good does it do to know that my decaying body will become part of the planet? Once I die, I'm gone. What about my memory living on? That's baloney too. How many of us know the names of our great-great-grandparents? Groundless optimism always ends in cynicism and despair. That is the message of Ecclesiastes:

> The sun rises, and the sun goes down,
>   and hastens to the place where it rises. . . .
> All things are full of weariness. (Eccles. 1:5, 8)

Maybe paganism has a point. We are trapped in a daily grind that cycles through dragging ourselves out of bed in the morning, going to work, watching the clock until quitting time, rushing home either to the loneliness of an empty house or to the whining of children, eating dinner, watching TV, and then collapsing back in bed again—only to repeat the cycle. It's not long before you work up a good depression. The circle of life crushes us. Recall Orwell's summary of life: "One is prepared in the end to be defeated and broken up by life."[7]

The Hebrew View: A Journey of Hope

The story of Ruth is different. Like the story of Joseph, it begins badly, but then heads toward resurrection. The Hebrew prophets saw life not as a circle but as a line that curves upward. History is moving toward a great climax, toward the invasion of God that will change everything. The central thesis of the Hebrew Bible is, in the words of Robert Alter, "the rebellion . . . against the pagan worldview, which is locked into an eternal cyclical movement."[8] We are not trapped in a cycle of despair but are on a journey of hope.

Why did the Hebrews have a different view of life than other ancients had? The Israelites knew and experienced a God who incarnates, "who acts for those who wait for him" (Isa. 64:4). This isn't the same old story; it is new news, in fact, it is good news. That's what the New Testament writers called it—*good news*, or the Greek word translated "gospel." Scholars call the biblical view a linear view of history, but it is actually shaped like a J, beginning with life and then going down into death and then upward to resurrection, a J-curve. Jesus lives a J-curve (fig. 9.2). He describes his life as a seed dying and rising again (John 12:24). Gospel stories are possible only because God actively shapes history, bringing life where there is death. Because God has come to help us in the incarnation, life, death, and resurrection of Jesus, the cycle has been broken! If Christ is risen, then Orwell is wrong.

Figure 9.2. The "J-curve" of death and resurrection

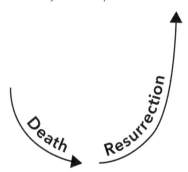

The book of Ruth is a gospel story.[9] A gospel story is a new way of looking at life. As stated in the introduction, almost every Disney animated movie is a death-resurrection story—a gospel story of sorts. As my six-year-old daughter Courtney pointed out, the plot follows the pattern of happy-sad-happy. The early church was so familiar with the shape of the gospel as a downward movement into death and then an upward movement into resurrection that they realized baptism was a symbol of that movement (Rom. 6:3–4; Gal. 3:27–28).

No story is more powerful than a gospel story. In fact, if you want to write a book or a movie script, you'd better make it a gospel story, or it likely won't sell. When *Troy* came out as a movie, I thought, "It will flop. It isn't a gospel story; it's a Greek tragedy." I was right. It flopped. *Les Misérables*, though, whether on Broadway, Public TV, or the big screen, is a hit. It's the power of the gospel.

Understanding Gospel Stories

Our hearts were made for gospel stories. The gospel story so gripped Paul the apostle that he wanted it to map his own life. He hungered to know the "fellowship of sharing in [Jesus's] sufferings, becoming like him in his death" so that he could experience the resurrection from the dead (Phil. 3:10, NIV).

As we've seen, the crucible for enduring love is suffering. Of course, we don't hunt for suffering—that's a heresy called asceticism—but we can't separate suffering from love. We've seen that repeatedly in the story of Ruth and Naomi. So our journey of love has a shape to it—like a J-curve. When we understand this framework, it resets our expectations for what life is like. In *hesed* love we enter into the dying-resurrection life of Jesus.

I am constantly inviting people into gospel stories, usually when they are at the bottom of the J-curve. I have a friend who lives on the West Coast and takes care of his wife, who has had a mild stroke. Even before the stroke, their marriage was strained. My friend shared with me, "I don't love my wife. I'm not even sure I like her. I'm just dutiful." We talked together about God's pattern of teaching us to love by overloading our systems so we are forced to cry for grace. God permits our lives to become overwhelming, putting us on the downward slope of the J-curve so we come to the end of ourselves. I encouraged my friend to embrace the downward path, not to push against it or worry about where his feelings were with his wife. Jesus said, "The good shepherd lays down his life for the sheep. . . . No one takes it from me, but I lay it down of my own accord" (John 10:11, 18). Seeing the gospel as a journey remaps our stories by embedding them in the larger story of Jesus's death and resurrection. His normal becomes our normal.

Dying comes in many forms. One of our ministry's prayer seminars was particularly large, and I felt the pressure to perform, to be a prayer expert. I felt my soul corroding, so I asked God for help. At the end of the seminar, when a long line of people seeking counsel had formed, I realized the line was an answer to my prayer. God was giving me a hidden work of love to balance out the public ministry of teaching. I was spent, but the small amount of serving that came from loving when I was brain-dead did my soul a world of good.

As the line dwindled, I noticed a well-dressed woman in her forties waiting patiently at the end. She told me that life had been good. She had a challenging job that she enjoyed and she had traveled the world, but her heart was broken over never finding a husband. I was overwhelmed by her broken heart. I find that happens to me when I don't give in to either quick theological answers (saying, "God will provide") or cynicism (thinking, "Maybe he won't"). My heart does a mini-lament. So I prayed as I listened. But when she said, "My hands are bloodied from banging on the door of heaven asking for a husband," I knew what she had to do. She had to die to her dream. When our dream becomes a demand, it takes center place where only God should be. When I shared that with her, tears filled her eyes. She too knew she had to die to her dream. So I prayed for her, for grace to die, and if it pleased the Lord, that he would give her a husband.

I've deliberately chosen three stories of people at the bottom of the J-curve because that's where Ruth and Naomi are at this point in the story. We see hints of hope, but they are only hints at this point. So where's the resurrection? Here's what I have learned going through the J-curve:

1. We don't know how or when resurrection will come. It is God's work, not ours.
2. We don't even know what a resurrection will look like. We can't demand the shape or timing of a resurrection.
3. Like Jesus, we must embrace the death that the Father has put in front of us. The path to resurrection is through dying, not fighting.
4. If we endure, resurrection always comes. God is alive!

The Gospel as Journey

The commitment to love, like Ruth's commitment to Naomi, always draws us into a gospel story. The gospel is a proposition: "Jesus died on the cross for my sins." But it is a proposition embedded in a story—the story of Jesus's life, death, and resurrection. When Paul describes the gospel in 1 Corinthians 15:1–4, he tells a story of Jesus's life, death, and resurrection, a story with a shape—the J-curve.

In Philippians 2:1–11, Paul describes how to live in a J-curve. As we go downward into death, we are active: active in seeking humility, in taking the lower place, in mindless, hidden serving. This is the journey Jesus took. The words that describe what Jesus did are action words. He *emptied* himself. He *took* the form of a servant. He *was born* in the likeness of men. He *humbled* himself by becoming obedient to the point of death. We can do death. But we can't do resurrection. We can't demand resurrection—we wait for it.

The humility we've seen in Ruth is not secondary to the gospel. It is the path of the gospel, the J-curve. It is the footpath that a gospel-centered journey takes. If you see the gospel only as a proposition that you believe, that reshapes your identity, you can easily slip into a kind of gospel narcissism where "Jesus for me" just makes you touchy. You've never moved on from Jesus's death for you to your death for others. Jesus is good for your self-image, but he hasn't mastered your life. He doesn't own you.

Up to this point in the story, Ruth has been doing death, cheerfully pursuing the bondage of love. Loving like Jesus, based on faith in Jesus, gives us the joy of Jesus and sets us up for resurrection. So faith in Christ isn't just mental assent but also an entering into his life. It remaps my expectations of what life is like. It kills the grumps because it isn't you against me, but me living in the pattern of Christ's journey. Every low-level evil we encounter is a door into Christ.

So, when you let the other person have the last word in an argument, you join the J-curve. You die a little death as the other person wins in the lack of clarity hanging over the conversation. But in the silence of losing you find yourself tucked under the wings of God.

LOVE LANDS

Ruth's life continues to narrow as a consequence of her love for Naomi: "And Ruth the Moabite said to Naomi, 'Let me go to the field and glean among the ears of grain after him in whose sight I shall find favor.' And she said to her, 'Go, my daughter'" (Ruth 2:2).

The abruptness of the text suggests that Ruth gets up immediately. It is critical she not lose a day of working in the fields. Notice who isn't going out harvesting—Naomi.[1] Does that bother Ruth? No. Naomi is older but likely not more than forty-five or fifty. We're looking at another real-life demonstration of the cost of love. Remember, *hesed* doesn't look at the fairness of love; *its commitment has nothing to do with how the other person treats you.* This is the third time Ruth has demonstrated one-way love: when Naomi didn't thank Ruth after her commitment to stay with her, when Naomi ignored her at the city gates, and now. *Hesed* love cleans out all our wrong motivations for love because we get nothing in return, just more work. It is a real ego killer.

Did you notice that Ruth asks Naomi's permission to be her servant? Ruth never misses a beat. Love doesn't go through the day with a measuring stick, testy over the unevenness of life. Our undying, never-stopping love, reflects the Father's undying love for us in Christ Jesus. This call to radical love permeates the New Testament. Paul describes the follower of Jesus as walking "with all humility and gentleness, with patience, bearing with one another in love" (Eph. 4:2). We can get so lost in the details of Paul's great application chapters in Colossians 3–4 and Ephesians 4–6 that we miss the whole. Paul expects and assumes that the power of the cross brought to bear on the life of the believer through the filling of the Holy Spirit transforms us into 24-7 lovers.

By the way, Naomi appears to be depressed. That could explain her seeming listlessness. In our modern world, we look at depression as an illness to escape. But sometimes life is just depressing. Ruth doesn't judge Naomi for her inactivity. She just loves.

As Ruth ventures out, she doesn't know which field to go to, whether anyone will welcome her, and what risks she faces. All is unknown. Love puts us in similar situations. We aren't sure where we stand or how people will react. This discomfort tempts us to achieve a semblance of control. The pagan culture that surrounded Israel sought control by rigidly stratifying society and using religion as a means of controlling evil. In a dangerous world, the people wanted to reduce risk. Our modern culture's obsession with safety and perfection is little different. It too leaves us frozen, causing us to shut down or retreat.

So how do we get traction when so much could go wrong? How do we operate in ambiguity? No matter how fuzzy our circumstances, we can always love. We can do *hesed*. Our world may be ambiguous, but our calling isn't. Instead of fighting the uncertainty, we can love in it. Faith grows in the rich soil of ambiguity. Because everything is uncertain, we find ourselves praying our way through the day or through relationships. Walking with the Good Shepherd on this journey of love becomes like breathing. Do not put your energy into ordering what you cannot control; simply love in the disorder. That's what Ruth does.

Love Is Local

As Ruth walks out of the city gates she sees a large open field with seemingly random stone markers delineating field ownership: "So she set out and went and gleaned in the field after the reapers, and she happened to come to the part of the field belonging to Boaz, who was of the clan of Elimelech" (Ruth 2:3).

Ruth has to land somewhere, in a specific field, with a particular landowner. If you are bent on pursuing personal freedom, you remain frozen hunting for the perfect field, the perfect person. You never land. You have to commit to make love work. We don't love in general. We love someone, somewhere. Setting our affections on someone always means narrowing down. Election and love are inseparable. This goes against the spirit of our age, which prizes independence and perfection. *New York Times* columnist David Brooks observes:

> [College] graduates are told to: Follow *your* passion, chart *your* own course, march to the beat of *your* own drummer, follow *your* dreams and find *your*self. . . .
>
> But this talk is of no help to the central business of adulthood, finding serious things to tie yourself down to. . . .
>
> Most successful young people don't look inside and then plan a life. They look outside and find a problem, which summons their life. A relative suffers from Alzheimer's and a young woman feels called to help cure that disease. A young man works under a miserable boss and must develop management skills so his department can function. . . .
>
> Most people don't form a self and then lead a life. They are called by a problem, and the self is constructed gradually by their calling.
>
> . . . When you read a biography of someone you admire, it's rarely the things that made them happy that compel your admiration. It's the things they did to court unhappiness—the things they did that were arduous and miserable.[2]

Often our difficulties with love are simply that we react to the constriction that accompanies love. But that constriction is inherent in love. To love is to limit. The French novelist Françoise Sagan talks candidly about this loss of freedom. Toward the end of her life she was asked by an interviewer, "Have you lived the life you've wanted to live?" "Yes," Sagan said, "I've lived to be free." The interviewer queried, "Then you've had the freedom you wanted?" "Yes. Well, I was obviously not free when I was in love with someone, but one is not in love all the time fortunately. Apart from that, yes, I've been free."[3] What a sad life.

Ironically, the experience of love, of narrowing your life, broadens and deepens your life. The narrower your life, the broader your soul. I see this particularly in men who have learned to love one woman over the course of many years. These husbands develop enormous capacities for gentleness, thoughtfulness, and grace. Those who flee the sting of particularity often end up flat, without depth, lost in ephemeral things.

Love always involves a narrowing of the life, a selecting of imperfection. So God's love for us lands. It landed in Bethlehem sometime in the fall or winter of 5/6 BC as a little Jewish boy. God's love is so specific it boggles the mind.

Guided by an Unseen Hand

The Hebrew for the phrase "she happened to come to the part of the field belonging to Boaz" actually mentions chance twice. A more precise translation would be "as luck would have it, she chanced upon the field. . . ." The writer intended for this striking understatement to point out that an unseen hand was guiding Ruth from the moment she walked out of the house.[4]

The awareness of a master storyteller weaving my life lets me pause and, like an artist, see hidden blessings and patterns when I begin to bear the cost of narrowing my life. It lets me endure in love because I know Someone is guiding the story toward resurrection. I really can't imagine *hesed* love without God's unseen hand guiding and shaping the story. In fact, I am a complete idiot to do *hesed* love without a loving God orchestrating life. But if an unseen hand is shaping the day, then the day becomes an adventure. That frees me to do even repetitive and mindless work, like the harvesting Ruth will do today.

Reaping by hand was grueling work: the task was divided by gender.[5] The men did the more physically taxing work of crouching down and cutting small bunches of wheat with a small, stone sickle and the women followed, gathering the stalks into bundles.[6] Ruth does both. Widows like Ruth and Naomi were permitted to follow the reapers, collecting scraps. The law of Moses instructed the Israelites, "When you reap the harvest of your land, you shall not reap your field right up to its edge, neither shall you gather the gleanings after your harvest" (Lev. 19:9).[7] It was an ancient version of Food Stamps, except you had to work for your food.

Picture Ruth bending down and collecting individual stalks of grain in the hot sun—unthanked, unprotected, and unknown. This is the face of *hesed*.

Many years ago God designed a situation where I was demoted and given the job of fundraising. I'm not naturally a people person, and the frequent rejection I got was humbling. Every day I prayed Colossians 3:22–24: "Slaves, obey your earthly masters in everything; and do it, not only when their eye is on you and to win their favor, but with sincerity of heart. . . . It is the Lord Christ you are serving" (NIV). During those years when I read the book of Ruth, the pages would be wet with my tears. I had no future, no hope of a future, just the flimsy words of God that he would be with me.

I remember reading Psalm 34:18, "The LORD is near to the brokenhearted / and saves the crushed in spirit," and thinking, "I qualify. That's exactly how I feel." The text felt so weak. After all, it was just words. But it was all I had. As I endured in love, as I did the right thing with the limited resources God had given me, those flimsy words came alive with unbelievable power.

A Case for Helpfulness

We've been examining what *hesed* love feels like on the inside, in our hearts. That can get complex. But on the outside, with our hands, love is surprisingly simple. Ruth did something concrete for her mother-in-law that spring morning in 1100 BC. Ruth was helpful. There's not a lot of drama in helpfulness, but it is the fabric of love. Helpfulness is *hesed* in action. It is a quiet doing that fits the needs around you.

I'm struck by how many people fail at this. I think of Dennis, who was a brilliant programmer and, on the side, an equally brilliant investor. But his frugality kept him from buying an air conditioner for his wife. He never took the time to arrange date nights. He wasn't helpful. One day his wife up and left. She couldn't take it anymore. I wish Dennis had not been so principled ("need to save money"), or maybe had better principles and had just been helpful.

When I was writing *A Praying Life*, Bob Allums, our A Praying Life ministry director, encouraged me to make the book helpful. Instinctively, I wanted something more grandiose, but his word *helpful* struck a chord. It was so plain, so unpretentious. So every day I prayed as I wrote, "Lord, make this book helpful." I asked my friend David Powlison to pray that helpfulness would describe my life. The word *helpful* struck him as well, causing him to reflect that

> to be *helpful* is to be free—of messianic delusions, of pride, of condescension, of despair, of impossible burdens, of selfish withdrawal. Helpfulness is humble, caring, forgiving, and constructive in innumerable small ways. And "helpful" is the very best we can be for each other. "Bear one another's burdens" goes in both directions. Both need aid, both give aid. Helpful is what we see Jesus being in the Gospels. His timely words, constructive actions, noticing and paying attention, the pacing and tempo of his life—these didn't make it all better, but they made a difference. Jesus was helpful.[8]

Make us simply helpful to each other.

11

LOVE PROTECTS

Every time I endure in love, I go through a mini-death and mini-resurrection. To put it simply, God shows up. I can never predict how or when, but it is as clear as the computer screen in front of me. The place of dying love is the place I meet God. John says, "God is love, and whoever abides in love abides in God, and God abides in him" (1 John 4:16). And sure enough, God shows up for Ruth: "And behold, Boaz came from Bethlehem. And he said to the reapers, 'The Lord be with you!' And they answered, 'The Lord bless you.' Then Boaz said to his young man who was in charge of the reapers, 'Whose young woman is this?'" (Ruth 2:4–5).

A translation that captures the surprise in "behold" might be, "And wouldn't you know it, Boaz came from Bethlehem!"[1] Not only does Ruth "just happen" to arrive at Boaz's field, but it just so happens that Boaz shows up at the same time. These seeming coincidences reveal the Designer behind the story and thus renew our courage to endure in the story.

Ruth at Risk

Boaz's question, "Whose young woman is this?" is a perfect example of how non-Western cultures view community. We ask, "Who is that person?" but Boaz asks, "Whom does she belong to?" Doug Green, a Hebrew scholar, explains:

> In a non-western world people are never defined individually; they are always understood in relation to a group, be it a family, a village, or a clan. An unmarried woman derived her identity from her father. She was tied to domestic duties in her father's household until the day of her marriage. If she chose to live outside the authority and protection of her father she was deemed to be a harlot.[2]

In effect, Boaz is saying, "What clan is this woman part of? Who is the man who protects and provides for her?" The answer is no one. The following ranking of the social status gives us a sense of her vulnerability. Ruth is at the bottom:

1. King or judge of Israel
2. Tribal leader (Judah)
3. Clan leader (Bethlehem)
4. Clan-subgroup leader (Boaz's status, or number 3)
5. Older father
6. Father (Elimelech)
7. Eldest son
8. Son
9. Wife (Naomi)
10. Daughter
11. Male servant
12. Female servant
13. Female servant lower class
14. Resident alien[3]
15. Male foreigner
16. Female foreigner (Ruth's status)

Ruth has neither father nor husband, nor brother, nor son to protect her. And remember, she lives in Israel's Dark Ages. Judges 19 gives us an idea of how vulnerable women were. It describes in almost X-rated detail how a traveling Levite pushed his concubine outside to placate thugs who were banging on the door. They raped her all night, and the Levite found her dead on the doorstep in the morning.

In the ancient world, relationships were everything. Libbie Groves observes:

> The presence of a male represented more than protection. If a male was with Ruth, it declared her status and said that she was properly fitted into a family structure and was a respectable woman. She should be treated as such. If she was unaccompanied, it signaled that she was not a respectable woman. It was fine to treat her any way you chose. The presence of a male communicated that the family she belonged to cared enough about her not to send her out without a chaperone. If you messed with her, her family would come after you. If she was alone, then either she didn't have a family to protect her, or they didn't care about her, so you could probably molest her with impunity.[4]

Without a male protector, Ruth is sexually vulnerable; without money she is financially destitute; without a friend, she is lonely; and without her country, she is open to prejudice. She has no protector, husband, tribe, family, or food. And she is shouldering the responsibilities of a man. She is one gutsy lady. Vulnerability is part of the cost of *hesed*. Love carries risk.

Usually when we think of courage, we think of something dramatic, but in my experience, most acts of courage are hidden, like Ruth's venturing out to the field alone. Courage is the sinew of love, the relational equivalent of foot washing. Or think for a moment of Jesus's teaching in the Sermon on the Mount: "If you . . . remember that your brother has something against you . . . go. First be reconciled to your brother" (Matt. 5:23–24). Even if it isn't my fault, even if I might get an earful, I must pursue the problem. So if a family member is tense or irritable, and I am tempted to let it blow over, Jesus tells me to pursue my "brother" with questions, such as, "Is something the matter?" That's courage.

Love Displays Us

The answer Boaz gets from the foreman is that this woman is highly vulnerable.

> And the servant who was in charge of the reapers answered, "She is the young Moabite woman, who came back with Naomi from the country of Moab. She said, 'Please let me glean and gather among the sheaves after the reapers.' So she came, and she has continued from early morning until now, except for a short rest." (Ruth 2:6–7)

Ruth's character leaps out of the foreman's description. She has been working from early morning with only a short rest.[5] She jumps at the problem of hunger by leaving immediately for the harvest with the same quiet and quick determination she demonstrated when she offered her life to Naomi. Hebrew writers, like good artists, seldom tell us what a character is like. Instead, they show us. We discover Ruth by watching her encounter life. In Ruth we see a rare combination of confidence and humility. She makes herself vulnerable out of love when she herself is suffering, and she does it cheerfully, quietly, and without demand. She is a jewel.

Ruth breaks the mold of both ancient and modern definitions of femininity. She rejects the dark side of feminism with its tendency to seek self-fulfillment and the relational testiness that can come from victimhood. In short, she rejects rebellion and accepts the shape of the world that God has put her in. But she also rejects the dark side of conservatism, of traditional culture, that can oppress women with mindless servitude and marginalization. She moves out in the face of evil. She isn't paralyzed by her circumstances. Her faith in God leads to a robust doing.

> The wicked flee when no one pursues,
>> but the righteous are bold as a lion. (Prov. 28:1)

Ruth is a lioness!

Boaz's *Hesed* of Ruth

Having done his homework, Boaz now approaches Ruth out in the open field.

> Then Boaz said to Ruth, "Now, listen, my daughter, do not go to glean in another field or leave this one, but keep close to my young women. Let your eyes be on the field that they are reaping, and go after them. Have I not charged the young men not to touch you? And when you are thirsty, go to the vessels and drink what the young men have drawn." (Ruth 2:8–9)

Multiple barriers separate Ruth—a disconnected, poor, female, Moabite foreigner—from Boaz—a connected, wealthy, male, Israelite clan leader. He breaks through all those barriers with one word, "daughter." This word also suggests that Boaz is a generation older than Ruth.

When you become wealthy, as Boaz is, it is easy to lose an awareness of the detailed needs of the poor. When your needs are taken care of automatically, it's difficult to incarnate, to step into someone's shoes. Money naturally tends to elevate and separate us. Not so with Boaz. He envelops Ruth in his community with seven crisp commands:

1. Do not glean in another field.
2. Do not leave this one.
3. Keep close to my young women.
4. Let your eyes be on the field that they are reaping.
5. Go after them (the young women).

6. Have I not charged the young men not to touch you?
7. When you are thirsty, go to the vessels and drink.

Think of the difference between the clarity of Boaz's specific directions and, "Hey, feel free to stay in my field." If you are a newcomer, a general welcome leaves you uncertain. You don't know whether the person means it or is just being polite. If the person does mean it, you don't know how far the welcome extends, so you hesitate.

Boaz's words are carefully crafted to care for Ruth. The first five commands all say the same thing with slightly different nuances. For Ruth, a new person on a new job in a new culture, each repetition deepens the reassurance and the safety. In effect, Boaz is telling her, "Do not even think about leaving this field."[6] By the time he is finished, Ruth realizes he means it. Boaz's insistent generosity is a rare jewel.

By commanding instead of offering, Boaz protects Ruth emotionally. She doesn't have to sit there wondering what to do. Nor do the workers. His words are likely public, making it clear to the community that Ruth is "in," thus protecting her from jealousy and molestation. Boaz's wraparound care is simply astonishing. Libbie Groves summarizes:

> When Boaz told Ruth not to go to another field to glean, he is saying more than simply, "Hey, I have plenty. Save yourself a few steps and just do your one-stop shopping here. I don't mind sharing, so don't feel as if you're imposing." He is recognizing how much she is at risk and is saying, "You will be safe here. I hereby invite you into my sphere of protection, and as long as you stay in my fields you will not be harmed." As modern westerners we miss his extreme generosity.[7]

Love Protects Purity

After taking care of her hunger, Boaz cares for Ruth's purity by encouraging her to stay close to the women reapers. His question, "Have I not charged the young men not to touch you?" is a Hebrew way of saying that he is about to tell or already has told the young men not to touch her.[8] The wrath of this powerful man will come down on any guy who gets close to Ruth. "You mess with her, you mess with me." Boaz has a zero-tolerance policy.

Boaz doesn't trust young men. In fact, no one in the ancient world trusted young men. Traditional culture protected young women's purity like a precious jewel. A young woman only offered herself sexually when a man had committed himself publicly to *hesed* love—in other words, marriage. Being sexually intimate outside of marriage is like giving a stranger the title for your car and hoping he will eventually pay the cost. We would never do with a car title what many young women do with their bodies. Sexual intimacy is not a path to love; it is a seal for love.

Tim Keller, bestselling author and pastor, summarizes the Christian view of sexual intimacy:

> Sex is a unitive act. It is a way of saying, "I belong exclusively to you." After two people have given one another their whole life in a public covenant, sex seals that commitment. It's like glue, a way of creating deep intimacy between two people who say, "All the rest of my life belongs to you." If you have sex outside of marriage, then you are saying, "I want your body and I want to give you my body, but I don't want to give you the rest of my life. I don't want to give you myself legally, psychologically, or permanently. Let's give each other our bodies but keep our lives to ourselves. Let's stay independent."[9]

In contrast, our culture encourages young women to give away their best gift, their sexuality, for free as a way to get men to deepen a relationship and then commit. Hollywood relentlessly tells no-consequence stories showing sexual intimacy leading to committed love. In this false trajectory, *feeling love* is invested with almost divine power. The false trajectory that destroys purity goes like this:

Feeling love ➪ sexual intimacy ➪ loss of feeling ➪ discarded relationship

Finding fulfillment through *feeling love* is the great hope of our modern culture—and it is pure foolishness. Men take this best gift and then discard their girlfriends once the cost of love begins to weigh on them, leaving their former companions emotionally abused and alone. What was meant as a seal for *hesed* love becomes a temporary source of feeling good that ultimately destroys both sexes and leaves children fatherless.

In contrast, the biblical trajectory puts public commitment of *hesed* love before sexual intimacy:

Feeling love ➪ public commitment ➪ sexual intimacy ➪ enduring love

Dietrich Bonhoeffer summarizes this beautifully in a letter from prison: "It is not your love that sustains the marriage, but . . . the marriage that sustains your love."[10] That is, the *hesed* commitment provides the frame for feeling love and sexual intimacy. In contrast, sexual intimacy before commitment is devastating. Writer Kate Bolick interviewed five young female college graduates immersed in the hookup culture (sex without commitment). She writes: "This surprised me. . . . I asked if they wanted to get married when they grew up, and . . . they answered 'yes.' . . . 'I don't think I can bear doing this for that long!' whispered one."[11] What this young woman couldn't bear was the constant auditioning through sexual intimacy that leads nowhere.

Meg Jay, a psychologist writing in the *New York Times*, unwittingly touches on the ancient wisdom of the biblical trajectory when she describes "clients who wish they hadn't sunk years of their 20s into relationships that would have lasted only months had they not been living together." Bottom line, the guys choked at the public commitment to *hesed* love. Reflecting on why couples who cohabitate before marriage have higher divorce rates, Jay writes, "A life built on top of 'maybe you'll do' simply may not feel as dedicated as a life built on top of the 'we do' of commitment or marriage." One of Jay's clients, Jennifer, "said she never really felt that her boyfriend was committed to her. 'I felt like I was on this multiyear, never-ending audition to be his wife.'"[12]

The biblical trajectory, by maintaining purity, keeps the person whole. In contrast, the false trajectory, by separating sexual intimacy from commitment, fractures not only the relationship but the person. Notice how the dating partners of Kate Bolick fracture themselves when they separate *hesed*-like commitment from sex. Bolick describes

> the prominent academic who announced on our fifth date that he couldn't maintain a committed emotional relationship but was very interested in a physical one. Or the novelist who, after a month of hanging out, said he had to get back out there and tomcat around, but asked if we could keep having sex anyhow, or at least just one last time.[13]

She reflects further on the "hookup culture": "Depending on whom you ask . . . has either liberated young women from being ashamed of their sexual urges, or forced them into a promiscuity they didn't ask for. Young men, apparently, couldn't be happier."[14] Which is why Boaz didn't trust his young men.

Boaz's thoughtful finishing touch, "when you are thirsty, go to the vessels and drink what the young men have drawn," not only cares for Ruth's physical thirst, but is also symbolic. Drinking vessels are a big deal in cross-cultural tension. The Samaritan woman in John 4 was shocked that Jesus was willing to put his lips on her drinking vessel. In the American South in the 1950s there were separate drinking fountains for whites and blacks. By inviting Ruth to drink, Boaz isn't just quenching her thirst; he is welcoming her into community.

Love Begins with Looking

In less than a minute Boaz transforms Ruth's life. Overwhelmed, she throws herself to the ground, touching it with her forehead. Astonished at the extent of his care, she asks, "Why?": "Then she fell on her face, bowing to the ground, and said to him, 'Why have I found favor in your eyes, that you should take notice of me, since I am a foreigner?'" (Ruth 2:10).

Ruth's incredible sense of relief is our first window into her feelings. She is scared and clearly aware of her social standing as "a foreigner." Ruth underlines her aloneness by using a subtle pun that could be rendered, "You have noticed the unnoticed."[15] She is no plastic saint. She feels the cost of *hesed* love.

When you endure in love unnoticed, and someone notices, it can be overwhelming. You've held it in so long and gotten so used to the loneliness, it becomes your normal. So when love breaks through for you, when someone really cares, it bowls you over. Ruth's resurrection has begun. She's on the upward slope of the J-curve.

Notice also how important looking is to love. Ruth asks, "Why have I found favor in your *eyes*, that you should *take notice* of me?" Boaz uses the same language when he tells Ruth, "Let your *eyes* be on the field that they are reaping." In the Old Testament, action begins with the eyes.[16] So when Yahweh expressed his love for Israel, he told Moses, "I have surely *seen* the affliction of my people" (Ex. 3:7).

Paying attention is the first step of incarnation, of going into someone else's world. It is what Ruth has been doing with Naomi, and now for the first time someone does it with her. Boaz has entered Ruth's world. His path of *looking*, followed by *compassion*, followed by *action* protects Ruth from those who look in order to use or abuse.

Not surprisingly, the Gospels are filled with observations of Jesus looking at people. His looking was often followed by compassion and then action. Both the Good Samaritan and the father in the Prodigal Son follow this trajectory.[17] Instead of being frozen by the unknown, we can begin by looking. Instead of a plan, we have a path. So we don't have to figure everything out. That takes the pressure off.

12

THE WORLD MOVES
FOR LOVE

We left Ruth overwhelmed by Boaz's care for her. She had asked the obvious question, "Why?" Now Boaz explains, "All that you have done for your mother-in-law since the death of your husband has been fully told to me, and how you left your father and mother and your native land and came to a people that you did not know before" (Ruth 2:11).

Boaz has heard of Ruth's extraordinary kindness to Naomi and her courage in crossing cultural barriers. The phrase "you left your father and mother" is the same wording as Genesis 2:24, underlining that Ruth has forsaken marriage to love Naomi.[1] That report of her love matches perfectly the foreman's description of her, causing Boaz to delight in—to be honored by—her presence on his field. Ruth's love stuns Boaz. But it isn't just her love that Boaz sees. His language reflects God's call to Abraham to leave his parents and come to a land he did not know (Gen. 12:1). Boaz sees a faith in Ruth similar to Abraham's.

Boaz's alertness, which enables him to immediately notice a stranger in his field, cues him to be attentive to the story of Ruth in the village. After Naomi's entrance, the local women likely came to her home and brought gifts of food and drink and heard her story. Naomi would have told them how even back in Moab, Ruth had loved her in the midst of Ruth's own suffering. Ruth's love for Naomi has shocked the town. We sense Boaz reflecting, "So this is the woman everyone in Bethlehem was talking about!"[2] We get the feeling that he has just met a rock star of *hesed* love.

In M. Night Shyamalan's movie *The Village* a town elder says, "The world moves for love. It kneels before it in awe." *Hesed* love captivates us because it is so rare. When Mother Theresa spoke at Harvard, this little Albanian peasant woman got a five-minute standing ovation from the students and faculty. For what? For her love of the poorest of the poor. Now Boaz stands up and gives Ruth a one-man standing ovation, worshipping at the feet of love, in awe of Ruth.[3]

Experiencing Blessing on the Path of Love

After answering Ruth's question, Boaz blesses her, asking God to richly reward her—to bless her whole life: "The LORD repay you for what you have done, and a full reward be given you by the LORD, the God of Israel, under whose wings you have come to take refuge!" (Ruth 2:12).

Boaz's blessing contains two images. The first image is of repayment and reward. The word "repay" is derived from *shalom*, meaning "bountiful peace," where Ruth will be restored to wholeness. Practically, that means a loving husband, a house full of children, and abundant food.[4] The second phrase, "a full reward," is literally "may your wages be full." Behind Boaz's blessing is a sense that Ruth's love is a weight on God's heart that has accumulated like a divine debt, a debt so large that only God can repay it.[5]

Some are uncomfortable with the idea of reward, and wages for love smacks of manipulation and seems to undercut grace. They fear that people will love for the reward, for what they can get out of it. However, both Jesus and Paul frequently used the language of wages and reward. They knew that the universe is connected in unseen ways, that what we do today is connected to the rest of our lives. Life is a path or pilgrimage. It is lived not in isolated moments, but in trajectories of reaping and sowing. Everything we do now creates the person we are becoming. We do not live in an impersonal, rigid world in which obedience mechanically dispenses reward; we live in our Father's world, a richly textured world organized around invisible bonds that knit us together. All of life is covenant.

Our neglect of this truth creates cheap grace, where grace is disconnected from the shape of life. After explaining the gospel to the Galatians, Paul says, "Do not be deceived: God is not mocked, for whatever one sows, that will he also reap" (Gal. 6:7). In other words, "Don't think that grace has changed the moral shape of the universe." In Boaz's view, Ruth has done the spiritual equivalent of buying an initial offering of Apple or Microsoft stock. Boaz knows God. It is just a matter of time before Ruth's life is going to be soaked with blessing. Resurrection is in the air.

Boaz's vision of God as a rewarder and tender protector sharply contrasts with Naomi's view of God as an incompetent cosmic ruler. Boaz's blessing is God's gentle answer to Naomi's lament.

But Boaz does more than point to God as a rewarder. Boaz himself rewards Ruth, thus answering his own prayer, first physically and then emotionally. As a follower of Yahweh, he feels the obligation of Yahweh to love. The result? Boaz's words match his life. When that happens you have integrity, true authenticity.

The second image Boaz uses in his blessing is of Ruth hiding under the wings of God. Rural cultures know well the image of chicks hiding under the wings of a mother hen. I still remember trying to catch little chicks as a kid at my cousin's ranch in Oregon. They would scurry underneath their mother's wings. I'd back off because I didn't want the hen to peck me. This tender image pictures God's total care. Boaz is saying that God is going to hold Ruth close, warm, right next to his heart. Boaz's first image of reward takes care of Ruth's exterior world. This image cares for her heart, her emotional life. Boaz is both powerful and tender, a rare combination. Even the images in his blessing mirror his life.

Boaz's second image is not just a blessing; it is also a description of what Ruth has done. When Boaz says, "under whose wings you have come to take refuge," he puts his finger on the hidden power of Ruth's love, her faith. Ruth has asked Boaz what motivates his care for her. He answers by saying he is motivated by what motivates her—the God of Israel. Ruth doesn't follow Yahweh because that is part of the Naomi-love package. Ruth's whole being is hidden in God. That is the essence of faith. In the storm of *hesed* love, you hide yourself in God. He is your only refuge when you are enduring alone, without help. Faith is not a feeling—it is a place where you hide, close to the heart of God.

The Lost World of Blessing

Our deeply secular era sees blessings as merely polite speech. Not so the book of Ruth. It presumes the existence of a Mind, a divine presence, ordering our lives for good, for blessing. The first and last words of the book are blessings. Ten different times different people, or groups of people, bless one another, which suggest that the author wants to tell us something about blessings.[6]

In the West we are more familiar with negative blessings, or curses, than we are with the idea of blessing. A curse is a prayer that something would go wrong. It uses the power of words to try to destroy. A blessing, however, uses the power of words to create. It is a prayer, a request for God in his mysterious way to bring good into another person's life. A blessing (or a curse) assumes that (1) words have power and (2) our world is connected in unseen ways. For the Hebrews a blessing assumed that God is an active player in the universe, that human words spoken to God release God's creative power for good.[7]

In the face of the discouragement that so often colors our lives, a blessing is an encouragement. Jesus often encouraged people before he healed them. Before he brought the widow of Nain's son to life (Luke 7:13), he encouraged her with, "Do not weep." A blessing isn't just feel-good words or a way of being polite; it is divine energy doing work. It provides a gift that the giver can't afford, bridging the gap between my large desire and my small ability, and connecting the person blessed with God's even larger desire and larger ability. A blessing does something. It is the leading edge of love.

The how and why of a blessing is opaque. It is easy to chalk up blessings to "luck" or "talent." Because we can't see the cause, we assume there is none. But all the best things of life like love and hope are unseen. So it is with the presence of God. The psalmist says about God,

> Your way was through the sea,
> your path through the great waters;
> yet your footprints were unseen. (Ps. 77:19)

Jesus tells us that God's activity is like the wind that "blows where it wishes, and you hear its sound, but you do not know where it comes from or where it goes" (John 3:8). In order to discern the wind, you need to slow down and watch the story.

We don't take blessing seriously because the eighteenth-century

Enlightenment divided the world into the nonreal spiritual and the real physical: if you can't measure something, then it isn't real. That relegated blessings to the world of Santa Claus and Frosty the Snowman. Blessings are just happy thoughts that we send in someone's direction.

If there is no God (atheism) or if God is distant (deism), then blessing someone is just meaningless happy talk. But if a sovereign and loving God is shaping our lives, then to bless someone is to pray that the energy of God would come into their lives. We used to do this regularly in the West before the demise of Christianity. We said to one another, "God be with you," which got shortened to "good-bye."

Don't look at blessings as warm words to make someone feel better. This isn't Oprah. A blessing is asking the living God *to act*, to incarnate. It is an act of mini-creation. My daughter Courtney put it this way: "I think of blessing as mimicking our Creator in calling for things to be that are not yet. It is more than wishing—it is invoking the goodness of God to be made manifest—and to be the hands that manifest it."

Knowing that God's blessing is real gives us the courage to move out boldly, even in the face of overwhelming life circumstances. At one of the lowest points of my life, when my future had disappeared, I was passed over for director of a nonprofit I'd helped build. I went to the installation of the new director struggling with feelings of shame and hopelessness. I sought the new director out—a wonderful, godly man—greeted him warmly, and wished God's richest blessing on his ministry. I meant it. I wanted him to do well. He was visibly taken aback. The blessing had already begun to work. I was simply following Jesus's command to bless our enemies. This man was not my enemy, but the principle still stood.

In the face of overwhelming discouragement, when everything seems to be against us, we can offer someone a simple prayer, wishing another person good. Following Jesus in this way actively undermines a Grinch-like approach to life. We simply do not have to be frozen by evil.

13

HUMILITY:
THE PATH OF LOVE

Ruth was afraid when she walked into Bethlehem and then ventured out into the fields alone. She felt the cost of love. Now, she responds to Boaz's blessing of her with what sounds like a "great, joyous sigh of relief after the days of uncertainty since her husband's death":[1] "Then she said, 'I have found favor in your eyes, my lord, for you have allayed my fears and spoken kindly to your servant, though I am not one of your servants.'" (Ruth 2:13).[2]

In Hebrew the phrase "spoken kindly to your servant" literally means "spoken upon the heart." Picture talking to someone while laying your head on his or her heart. Ruth, with all her quiet power, feels Boaz's "sweet, caressing words."[3]

Earlier Ruth expressed amazement at Boaz's kindness because of the ethnic barrier ("that you should take notice of me since I am a foreigner"). In the passage above she is astounded that he cares for her despite their class differences ("though I am not one of your servants"). She uses the word *shipkhah*, a female servant of the lowest rank.[4] In essence she says, "I'm not even the lowest of the low." Ruth's act of loving put her at the bottom of society, but she doesn't push back on her lowered status. She accepts the cost of love. Like Jesus, she *takes the lower place.* Love and humility are inseparable.

When serving is combined with humility, the serving becomes almost pleasurable. You are thankful for any gift given you. In contrast, pride can't bear the weight of unequal love. Imagine a very different Ruth with a modern, victim-fed attitude. She comes to the field seething at Naomi for ignoring her yesterday and not helping her today, and irritated at God that he has put her in a situation where she is alone and vulnerable. So when Boaz offers to help, she is only grudgingly thankful, since he doesn't know how hard her life is or what she's given up. How could his small gifts ever make up what she's lost? Her simmering bitterness, her wounded sense of injustice, saps the joy out of life. Pride makes others' joy, or even the possibility of our own joy, feel phony. It is an odd sort of authenticity where we demand that others be as depressed as we are.

What is the impact of Ruth's dialogue on Boaz? Just like Naomi on the road to Bethlehem, Boaz is left speechless. "Even in deference she still had the last word."[5] Humility and love have almost a physical power that catches people by surprise and leaves them silent. That's what happened to Frances Russell when he heard Mother Teresa speak at Harvard:

> In the fading afternoon, I sit and listen. To love one another, to love one's children born and unborn, to love the poor—it is all so impossibly simple. "We can't do for all," she tells us. "So let us begin with one. Love to be true has to hurt." So she talks, that tough and indefatigable woman who began by scraping the dying from the Calcutta streets. She tells now of reaching out to a man she found lying in a gutter and his saying to her simply that it was the first time he could remember the warmth of a human hand. And I, the non-Catholic, sit there with my aging classmates, the tears running down my cheeks.[6]

Using Power for Love

By using his power for love, Boaz is drawn down into need. That's what humility does. It goes lower. Boaz gets to know someone at the bottom of society. Because he goes lower he gets closer. He uses his power to protect Ruth from the young men who are tempted to separate power from love by taking advantage of her under the guise of love.

Jesus also refuses to separate power from love. Each of the temptations in the wilderness seeks to get Jesus to use his power for self, but he refuses to use divine power to turn a stone into bread, to use his divinity to protect him from the full implications of his humanity. The temptation to jump from the highest point of the temple is a sign that has nothing to do with love, even if it would show the thousands of worshippers crowded into the temple that Jesus is truly the Son of God. The Pharisees continually ask Jesus for a sign, a spectacular miracle that will show the world who he is. It is power without love. Jesus would become an instant celebrity. No need for the cross. But what seduces us revolts Jesus. He tells the Pharisees, "An evil and adulterous generation seeks for a sign" (Matt. 16:4).[7]

Boaz is also attentive. Down low, you see better. As Ruth perceived the core of Naomi's problem, so Boaz sees to the core of Ruth. Others see a Moabite woman taking their grain; he sees a faith celebrity living a life of sacrificial love.

Ruth's humility continues to emerge in the story.

Love Includes

Imagine the next scene as a twelfth-century-BC high school lunch room. You are in the middle of eighth grade, and your family has decided to move. You leave your friends and go to a new school. What is the worst part of your day? Lunchtime! It is the one unstructured part of the day when the group that accepts you means everything. So where do you sit? What are you feeling?

Boaz, ever the protector, anticipates Ruth's angst: "And at mealtime Boaz said to her, 'Come here and eat some bread and dip your morsel in the wine.' So she sat beside the reapers, and he passed to her roasted grain. And she ate until she was satisfied, and she had some left over" (Ruth 2:14).

The Hebrew for "she sat beside the reapers" suggests that Ruth sat down at the side of or next to the reapers. Even when invited inside, she humbly took her place at the edge.

It is worth pausing and reflecting on the nature of humility.

1. *Humility is physical.* It involves a physical placement that is, in some way, lower.
2. *You can see humility.* It is not vague. We see humility in Ruth's thankfulness as she talks to Boaz, when she asks Naomi's permission to glean, when she throws herself at Boaz's feet in gratitude, and when she sits at the edge of the group.
3. *It can feel like you are disappearing.* When you are humble, people don't notice you.
4. *Many sins such as anger, jealousy, and quarreling are rooted in our unwillingness to take the low place.* When others treat us badly, they are

usually putting us in a low place, so we lash out because we don't like the low place.

5. *Once you get over the shock, the low place is a place of deep soul rest.* In Psalm 131 David describes his life in the low place where, he says, "my eyes are not raised too high." There, he says, "I have calmed and quieted my soul, / like a weaned child with its mother" (Ps. 131:1–2).

6. *You discover people in the low place.* It is like entering a darkened room full of friends. At first, you think you are alone, you can't make out anyone, but then as your eyes adjust to the light, you begin to see friends everywhere, maybe people that you didn't notice when you were up higher.

7. *The great joy of the low place is that it is where God dwells* (Isa. 57:15). When Jesus told us to "take the lowest place" (Luke 14:9), he was quoting Proverbs 25:6–7. His whole life was a lowering of himself (Phil. 2:1–11). Even if someone puts us in a low place, we can make the decision to go there. We can accept what God has brought into our life. When we make the choice to take the lower place, "you against me" becomes "God with me." This is what Ruth does by taking her seat at the edge.

Boaz's lunchtime invitation does for Ruth socially what his earlier directives did physically. His series of crisp, public commands directs Ruth into the heart of the community. He personally serves her, almost hovering over her, attending to her needs. It's almost embarrassing.

Boaz's clear commands eliminate any ambiguity and give Ruth a clear path to follow, thus penetrating the impervious shell of close-knit communities. Imagine the captain of the football team inviting you to sit with him at lunch and sharing his sandwich with you. Others might be jealous, but no one is going to mess with the high school icon.

The verb *passed* in "passed to her roasted grain" is used only here in the Old Testament, so we are unsure of its meaning. The Septuagint (the 200 BC Greek translation of the Hebrew Bible) actually coins a word here to say that Boaz *heaped* food in front of Ruth. That would make sense since she has food left over. Historically, a Middle Eastern guest would not finish his or her food because to eat all the food would imply that the host didn't offer the guest enough to eat. This understanding is implicit in Jesus's parable of the friend at midnight, where the host asks a neighbor for three loaves of bread, more than he needs. Boaz wants Ruth to feel the full weight of his love, to be filled to overflowing. He quietly and decisively counters Naomi's lament that she came back empty.

In the ancient Near East, the act of eating together established a bond, if not a covenant, between individuals. People could only honor, and never harm, someone with whom they ate. However, males and females never ate together, except in their immediate families. Boaz was breaking culturally accepted bounds by extending an invitation to a woman, and particularly by serving her.[8] The only other reference in the Old Testament to a man serving is to Abraham serving his divine guests (Gen. 18:1–8). But they were three celebrities (God plus two angels!). Ruth was a poor Moabite.

Boaz's lunch looks forward to Jesus's feeding of the five thousand, when the people would eat until they were full and had an abundance left over (Mark 6:42–43). The same pattern continues in the Last Supper, in Communion, and ultimately in the wedding feast of the Lamb. Looking forward to the wedding feast, Jesus said about himself, "He will dress himself for service and have them recline at table, and he will come and serve them" (Luke 12:37). Like Boaz, Jesus will hover over his bride, attentive to her needs, filling her glass, eager to serve her.

Like Jesus, Boaz loves to love. "Boaz took an ordinary occasion and transformed it into a glorious demonstration of compassion, generosity, and acceptance—in short, the biblical understanding of hesed."[9] Boaz is continuing the celebration that he started when he first greeted Ruth. *Hesed* love isn't just doing love; it is the enjoyment of love. It likes to have parties.

Love Reveals the Man

Far from disappearing—our great fear about humility—Boaz's humble serving reveals the man. From the point of view of traditional cultures, Boaz's serving of Ruth is incredible. Men usually don't serve women in traditional cultures. They fear they will lose their dignity if they enter a woman's world. Had Boaz treated Ruth this way, he would have left her alone and vulnerable.

In liberal cultures, such as our own, men are so concerned to treat women as equals that they don't serve them. Men become passive, almost spineless with women. Had Boaz been this way, he would have accepted Ruth but not been assertive in protecting or caring for her. Boaz's aggressive tenderness avoids both dangers. A real test of a man's character is how he treats women.

Boaz is a giver and protector of life. His eagerness to be generous, to seek out the need of someone who is so low, is striking. So many people seek the wealthy that the affluent can become overwhelmed and build barriers just for their sanity. Without realizing it, they can use their power to separate themselves from love, which is why Boaz's insistent generosity is striking. One scholar puts it this way: "From the first time Boaz opens his mouth until the last words he utters (4:9–10), his tone exudes compassion, grace, and generosity. In the man who speaks to this Moabite field worker biblical *hesed* becomes flesh and dwells among humankind."[10] That's authentic manhood.

And Boaz does not shy from the responsibility of leadership, visiting the field in the hot part of the day and staying with his workers. By first cautioning and then later directing the young men to generosity, he anticipates problems. In just a few hours he issues fourteen separate commands to care for Ruth. Hidden behind that drive is moral courage.

Ronald Reagan knew the power of moral courage when, standing in front of the Berlin wall, he told his Soviet counterpart, "Tear down this wall." Knowing Ruth's vulnerability, Boaz openly commands his workers to protect her purity. Often the love of money can freeze leaders from sticking their necks out ("I don't want to offend my best, productive workers.") But God's law has mastered Boaz. It is a reflex of his heart. In a world dominated by men, Boaz tells the young men to "stand down" to protect a vulnerable woman. He is diligent, engaged, and present. Like Ruth, Boaz comes alive as he loves.

LOVE CREATES COMMUNITY

When Ruth gets up from lunch, Boaz instructs his young men privately: "When she rose to glean, Boaz instructed his young men, 'Let her glean even among the sheaves, and do not reproach her. And also pull out some from the bundles for her and leave it for her to glean, and do not rebuke her'" (Ruth 2:15–16). We can tell Ruth was the first one up because only after she "rose to glean" did Boaz talk to his young men. The narrator continues to let us discover Ruth, not by telling us what she is like, but by showing us her character.

Boaz directs his workers to actually pull out grain from among the sheaves, implying that he wants them to be covertly generous. By welcoming Ruth and caring for her, he has followed the letter of the law. But his new command shows that he had grasped the heart of the law, which is to "love your neighbor as yourself" (Lev. 19:18). He starts by calculating his tithe; now he's pulling money out of his wallet by the fistfuls. Boaz wants to overwhelm Ruth with love. When God has blessed you with wealth, it is easy to be initially generous but then pull back because you are afraid you'll be trapped in giving. Not Boaz. He does the opposite.

Why does Boaz deepen his generosity? We don't know, but something powerful about *hesed* evokes love in others. It is more than imitation. *Hesed* love draws you in. It seduces you. You want to own its beauty, to enter it. Ruth's love draws Boaz, and he wants to draw his workers in as well, inviting them to become lovers, creating a chain of love. Jesus describes the same chain of love in John 15:9: "As the Father has loved me, so have I loved you. Abide in my love." Jesus's Passion is like that. It creates a whole new standard of love for the early church, leading to viewing martyrdom as a prize. Likewise, Ruth's love creates a new standard for Boaz. It disrupts his world; in fact, it disrupts the city of Bethlehem. Remember, life is lived in trajectories, not in isolated moments. Seeing Ruth's love, Boaz deepens his own trajectory of love, invites others into it, and actively works at forestalling a counter-trajectory of evil.

Hesed Love versus Defensive Love

By asking his workers to proactively include Ruth, Boaz risks their jealousy. Jealousy is extraordinarily deceptive. It is by far the most destructive sin in communities and organizations that I've been a part of, and yet, I seldom hear it mentioned or confessed. It always masks itself as something else, creating a hidden chain of slander that drags someone down. A multiheaded hydra, it begins with an inability to rejoice with another's success, leaks out as gossip, and finally erupts as slander. Jealousy seeks to gain by destroying others, while *hesed* loses by giving itself. One is the heart of evil. The other is pure gospel. The ninth commandment ("You shall not bear false witness") and tenth ("You shall not covet") are aimed at the heart of jealousy. Milton in *Paradise Lost* speculated that jealousy was the root sin of Satan's rebellion.

In 1990 as I walked to the train station after work, I saw and repented of jealousy in my own heart. My repentance unleashed a new work of God within me that still reverberates in my life. On that walk, I realized I was jealous of another mission's success. I repented by giving the mission that I worked for to God. That opened a door to giving my life in a new way in surrender to Jesus. I began repeatedly not only to surrender everything I owned to Jesus, but also to ask him to rule me completely. God took that prayer seriously by letting me experience suffering. It was his good gift to help me fall in love with his Son.

Boaz anticipates the problem of jealousy by ordering his workers not to shame Ruth. He reverses the normal, broken pattern by exposing jealousy and hiding love. He doesn't want to humiliate Ruth by making it look like she is taking charity, so he hides his giving. Jesus does that when he keeps the miracle at the wedding of Cana hidden. The young couple, instead of being embarrassed at their failure to have enough wine, are honored for their generosity in saving the best wine for last. If the focus had been on Jesus, the couple would look like a failure. Our best love is often hidden.

It would be easier for Boaz if he just gave Ruth extra grain quietly at the end of the day. He risks his workers' resentment because he wants to include her. In particular, his command "pull out some from the bundles" is directed toward the women because it is their job to create the bundles from what the men have cut. He wants the women to enter into his welcome of Ruth. He pushes the men away from her and the women toward her. By publicly giving Ruth food, he gives her not only food but also friends, thus covering her with his wings.

What is the likely effect on his harvesters as they stealthily pull stalks out of the sheaves and drop them on the ground? It would transform the day, making it almost fun. The boss is encouraging them to give away his stuff. They look good, and it doesn't cost them anything! The result? Ruth is included.

The Problem of Community

We've just watched Boaz welcome an outsider into community. Our modern quest for community has a thousand faces to it: Where can I go to find a place where I am loved? How can the church be a real community and not just a social club? How do I achieve intimacy in marriage? (Intimacy is just a state of heightened community on a small scale.)

Instinctively, we know what makes for a good community: a safe place where I am included, where I am known and loved, and I in turn know and love others. Creating an inclusive community is the holy grail of modern culture. But actually doing it is extremely difficult. The very qualities that create a tight-knit community work against including outsiders. It is like combining oil and water. That is, communities are almost always built around common interests or relationships. But the stranger by definition doesn't share those common interests. Why include someone when you don't understand one another?

All through our daughter Kim's schooling we struggled with her being excluded. Kim's autism can make it difficult to understand or connect with her, but with a little effort almost anyone can enjoy her. Sadly, the church was worse than the schools. At least in the schools with so many kids with disabilities, Kim's fellow students would warm to her. They would come up to her outside of school and say, "Hey Kim, remember me?" But most people in church avoided her. They didn't learn how to enjoy her. But disabilities like Kim's are the grains of sand that become the pearls of the community.

Jesus was proactive in creating inclusive communities. There was no other way; the inward pull of community was too strong. At one dinner party Jesus told the host that he had invited all the wrong people:

> When you give a dinner or a banquet, do not invite your friends or your brothers or your relatives or rich neighbors, lest they also invite you in return and you be repaid. But when you give a feast, invite the poor, the crippled, the lame, and the blind, and you will be blessed, because they cannot repay you. For you will be repaid at the resurrection of the just. (Luke 14:12–14)

The wounds in the body of Christ, the Moabites and the disabled, are actually to be celebrated and honored. When the world sees that, it sees Jesus. Authentic love is our most powerful argument for our faith.

The Secret to Creating Community

The biggest problem people have in searching for the perfect community is just that. You don't *find* community; you create it through love. Look how this transforms the way you enter a room of strangers. Our instinctive thought is, "Who do I know? Who am I comfortable with?" There's nothing wrong with those questions, but the Jesus questions that create communities are, "Who can I love? Who is left out?"

Instinctively, we hunt for a church or community that makes us feel good. It is good to be in a place where you are welcome, but making that quest central is idolatry. And like all idolatry, it ultimately disappoints. But if we pursue *hesed* love, then, wherever we go, we create community. Here are two different formulas for community formation:

> Search for community where I am loved ⇨ become disappointed with community

> Show *hesed* love ⇨ create community

The first formula leaves us critical and ultimately solitary. The second one enlarges our life, filling it with surprise. No matter what our situation—single, happily married, divorced, or in a difficult marriage—we can create community through love. We don't wait for love, we pursue it.

We do the same in marriage. The search for "true love," for intimacy, is the search for someone who will understand and care for me. There is much good in that desire, but once we discover that the other person is deeply flawed, we often pull back, thinking everything is wrong. A bad marriage is one where neither spouse does the hard work of love. But as soon as one spouse begins to do *hesed*, the bad marriage disappears. (I'm not saying this marriage is easy; just that it isn't somehow intrinsically flawed.) We are left with the good challenge of loving a difficult spouse.

We've unwittingly made the quest for community central. The quest for intimacy can be just a veiled request for feeling good. Intimacy and community come from love, not the other way around. So instead of pursuing intimacy, we should pursue love. Only then do we discover intimacy. That is what Ruth is doing. Ruth's living death for Naomi has created a powerful community between the two of them. John describes this pattern in Jesus's death: "[He] would die for the nation . . . to gather into one the children of God" (John 11:51–52). A dying love creates the possibility of oneness.

We push away the wounds in the body of Christ when these are the conduits of grace. The wounds might be a self-righteous spouse or a difficult child. Enduring in love with a headstrong husband or a self-righteous wife, living with an uneven love, creates community. I've seen that with my friend Peter, who visits his mildly schizophrenic wife in Michigan. I've watched him endure in love for twenty years now. After considerable struggles, both his daughters are happily married to believers, and one daughter is married to a pastor. I ran into one of his daughters, and she said, "Dad's enduring love saved our family." His endurance with his wife showed his daughters how to love when your world collapses.

After Jesus's resurrection he told Mary Magdalene, "I am ascending to my Father and your Father, to my God and your God" (John 20:17). Jesus's language echoes Ruth's ("Your God shall be my God") and alludes to the community he created by his death and resurrection.[1] Jesus's *hesed* of us, his broken body, created a new, broken community where we are bound together with him as fellow brothers and sisters. A dying love is the secret of all community formation.

Enduring in Love as a Single

What do you do if community—particularly marriage—is elusive, if your Boaz (or Ruth) never shows up? The decades-long assault on masculinity by our cultural elites is finally taking hold. Many men either are being seduced by the image of themselves as sports-obsessed and sex-crazed or are quietly retreating, fearful of commitment. Or both. They are great friends but lousy lovers. By lovers I mean *hesed* lovers who throw themselves with abandon into a life of committed love.

We are moving from a Promethean age of achieving big dreams to a Petronian age of listless cynicism. Petronius was Nero's director of entertainment and the author of the *Satryicon*, the story of two male lovers vying for the sexual favors of a young male. R. R. Reno says about Petronius:

> He is an observer who can mock and satirize. He can describe veniality without judgment; he can narrate vice without protest. . . . He creates a pervasive atmosphere of superficiality that drains all spiritual significance from events. His characters are realistic, yet they are spectral, soulless creatures who utterly lack gravity. Never moralistic, never injecting the voice of some loftier vision . . .

Reno goes on to describe how our culture embodies this change:

> Our postmodern culture . . . supports our desire to be invulnerable observers and not participants at risk. Petronian humanism wishes to neuter all power and potency. . . . no dynamism is allowed to penetrate the defenses of irony, satire, and critical sophistication. The soul must remain unaltered, unaffected.

If you inhale the spirit of our age, then instead of pride and power you have a new set of master sins with which to struggle:

> Sloth and cowardice . . . both slink away from the urgency of conviction. Both fear the sharp edge of demand and expectation. Both have a vested interest in cynicism, irony, and outward conformity. These vices, not pride, now dominate our culture.[2]

Consequently men are emasculated, fearful of commitment, and lovely young women are left alone. The solution? Encouraging men to image Boaz, to put away childish things by shutting down the video game and falling in love. This is not a list of duties but the beginning of a journey of *hesed* love that draws us into the J-curve, "the fellowship of sharing in his sufferings, becoming like him in his death" (Phil. 3:10, NIV).

We can easily forget that all Ruth's triumphs of love are done while she is single, without marriage prospects. In fact, her greatest triumph is embracing singleness as a way of caring for someone in a seemingly dead-end relationship.

Even though ancient cultures lauded marriage, Scripture celebrates singleness. The Bible's two greatest leaders, Jesus and Paul, were both single and encouraged singleness because of the freedom it gives someone to love on multiple fronts. Recent discoveries in archaeology suggest that Jesus was on friendly terms with the first-century Essene movement, in which single Jewish men and women lived communally. Circumstantial evidence suggests that Jesus's three single friends, Mary, Martha, and Lazarus, might have been associated with the Essene communities in Judea.[3] We may not be able to control the state we are in (single, married, divorced, widowed), but we can control our response to it. We can choose to reflect the beauty of Jesus.

The Presence of Jesus at the Heart of Community

At the heart of any lasting community is the presence of Jesus leading us into his dying-resurrection love, the Redeemer creating mini-redeemers. It looks like this:

Jesus's dying love for me ⇨ my dying love for others ⇨ community

Here's a simplified version of the same idea:

Faith ⇨ love ⇨ community

As we've seen, you can't get at community directly. If you do, you'll create not an inclusive community but a tribe that thinks and acts the same way. In marriage, if you pursue intimacy directly, you'll just become demanding and push your spouse away. Instead, you have to become a redeemer in your marriage through a dying love. That creates community.

Every morning when Kim and I have our prayer time, we have a little community together. I love sitting there, watching her pray, enjoying her prayers, and making suggestions when she gets stalled. She usually giggles through some of her prayers for angry people. I smile with her.

15

LOVE INVITES RESURRECTION

Ruth comes to the end of an exhausting but wonderful day.

> So she gleaned in the field until evening. Then she beat out what she had gleaned, and it was about an ephah of barley. And she took it up and went into the city. Her mother-in-law saw what she had gleaned. She also brought out and gave her what food she had left over after being satisfied. (Ruth 2:17–18)

To glean the barley, Ruth spreads out her all-purpose shawl on the ground, takes a handful of barley stalks, and strikes them with a stick, knocking the heads of grain onto the shawl (step 2 in fig. 15.1). Handful by handful she goes through the day's harvest, leaving a large pile of grain. Her pile—an ephah—is enormous. An ephah is about twenty-two liters, enough food for one person for at least half a month. She'll do steps 3 and 4 at the end of the harvesting season.

Figure 15.1. Stages of harvest

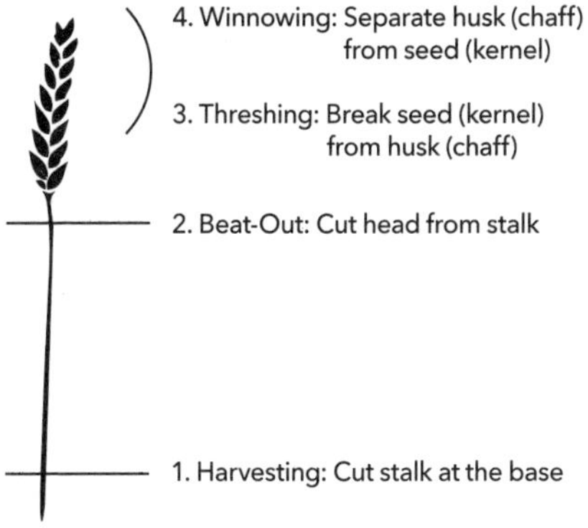

4. Winnowing: Separate husk (chaff) from seed (kernel)

3. Threshing: Break seed (kernel) from husk (chaff)

2. Beat-Out: Cut head from stalk

1. Harvesting: Cut stalk at the base

Ruth wraps the grain in her shawl, lifts it onto her back, and trudges back to the city late at night after working a sixteen-hour day. Given that grain was the ancient equivalent of income, "Ruth collected the equivalent of at least half a month's wages in one day."[1] We also discover that Ruth has saved her lunch leftovers for Naomi. You never catch Ruth not loving.

Naomi's Reaction

Naomi is shocked: "And her mother-in-law said to her, 'Where did you glean today? And where have you worked? Blessed be the man who took notice of you.' So she told her mother-in-law with whom she had worked and said, 'The man's name with whom I worked today is Boaz'" (Ruth 2:19).

Naomi is excited, almost animated, asking several rapid-fire questions without waiting for an answer, and jumping into a blessing of this unknown man.[2] She knows a man has cared for Ruth: "Blessed be the man who took notice of you." Ruth couldn't have gleaned that much grain without a male protector.

Ruth adds a touch of playful drama by tantalizingly saving Boaz's name until last: "The man's name with whom I worked today is . . . Boaz." Behind this mini-drama is a delightful double-irony: Naomi doesn't know that Ruth has worked in Boaz's field, and Ruth doesn't know who Boaz is![3]

God literally fills Naomi up. He provides not only a meal, but also a complete plan for the harvest time and protection for Ruth. God responds to Naomi's lament with love, not a lecture. He tenderly proves her wrong with an overwhelming generosity. God is doing *hesed* with Naomi, out-loving her grief.

By the way, how much help has Naomi given Ruth this day? Zip. Has she directed Ruth to Boaz's field? No. Has she told Ruth about Boaz? Nope. Loving in situations like this purifies you. It clears out your mixed motives because you aren't getting anything out of it. Self disappears as a motivation because nothing you do is helping you. Self dies. That leaves space for God to care for you when others don't. So once again we see that in the middle of a death, we should keep an eye out for resurrection.

Hesed Love Creates Resurrection and Change

When Naomi discovers that Boaz is the one who befriended Ruth, her tone changes even further as she breaks out in worship: "And Naomi said to her daughter-in-law, 'May he be blessed by the LORD, whose kindness has not forsaken the living or the dead!'" (Ruth 2:20).[4]

Naomi's phrase "the living and the dead" speaks to the heart of her tragedy, which is not just her devastating losses, but also that the sum of her losses means her family has died out. When Naomi learns that the man is Boaz, she immediately connects the dots. Ruth might marry Boaz, and so continue the line. God is showing *hesed* both to Naomi (the living) and to Elimelech (the dead). The ever-prudent Naomi keeps this possibility to herself.[5] Her silence allows Ruth to be completely herself.

Naomi's transformation is total: we see "an upward surge of her spirit, a lifting from the depths. . . . And we know that Naomi, who was herself among the dead, lives again."[6] Ruth's *hesed* love of Naomi created the possibility of this resurrection. God's *hesed* love of us by the gift of his Son gave us our resurrection as well. That's what love does. It creates the opportunity for resurrection.

Even though Naomi has named herself "bitter Naomi," God has not. In the Greek or pagan worldview people are locked into fixed descriptions, like Homer's "swift Ulysses." Paganism is rigid. Your label defines you. But because of the intrusion of God's grace, biblical characters are a "center of surprise"; they have the capacity for change.[7] So we never read about "angry Moses" or "wily Jacob."

Oddly enough, Christians have labeled Naomi "bitter Naomi." But neither our sin nor our environment defines us. We are not trapped by our own moodiness or despair. We can change because an infinite God is personally involved in the details of our lives. As bearers of God's image, we can cry out for mercy and see God act in our circumstances or in our hearts. Jesus's "judge not" is a call to give people space to change, to back off from locking in on exclusively negative views. Especially in long-term relationships, we run the risk of locking onto a person's negatives and going pagan on them.

A friend of mine, a special-ed teacher, had one of her second grade students labeled bipolar by a psychologist. That child will likely be stuck with that label. The result is that other teachers will view that child through that lens, and they will have a low expectation for his behavior. They see him not as a center of surprise who can change but as *bipolar*, trapped by a category of pop-psychology. When he misbehaves, he will be told he's bipolar, thus incapable of change. As the spirit of paganism rises in our culture, more and more people tend to think of their spouse as a category, as controlling-Sue or mean-Joe. While your spouse might be controlling or mean, your locking him or her in is a form of judging. We fail to see the other person as a center of surprise.

Our society has raised judging to an art form. To counter my heart's tendency to judge, I begin my daily prayers for Jill by thanking God for her. I have a prayer card jammed with ways that Jill reflects Jesus. I'm not trying to be balanced in how I look at my wife, I'm trying to rebalance my heart, which tends to go negative.

The Cure for a Cranky Soul

Naomi has a final caution for Ruth:

> And Ruth the Moabite said, "Besides, he said to me, 'You shall keep close by my young men until they have finished all my harvest.'" And Naomi said to Ruth, her daughter-in-law, "It is good, my daughter, that you go out with his young women, lest in another field you be assaulted." (Ruth 2:21–22)

Notice the subtle difference between Boaz's instruction, "keep close by my young *men*," and Naomi's, "go out with his young *women*." It is likely an innocent, generic comment on Boaz's part, but the ever-alert Naomi is keen on protecting Ruth's purity.

Imagine a modern, in-touch-with-myself reaction to Naomi's counsel: "I can't believe you are still ordering me around! You didn't offer to help me today or even tell me where Boaz's field was. Do you realize what could have happened to me? You left me with all the work, and now you're telling me who I can hang out with? I don't think so. I've given up everything for you and you won't even care for my future by letting me get to know some guys." Because it feels so real, so honest, and so passionate, cathartic blasting is almost iconic in our culture. It's imagined as a path to my inner peace and our relational intimacy, but it leads to neither.

It just destroys. The faux authenticity of self-righteous dumping is just a mask for enshrining my feelings, for doing my own thing.

You might think I've overstated the possibility of a grumpy response to Naomi's counsel. Maybe people were nicer back then. No, not really. In Jesus's parable of the lost son, when the father throws a lavish party for his wayward son, the older son's rant is similar to the imagined rant above: "Look, these many years I have served you, and I never disobeyed your command, yet you never gave me a young goat, that I might celebrate with my friends. But when this son of yours came, who has devoured your property with prostitutes, you killed the fatted calf for him!" (Luke 15:29–30). The human heart has remained unchanged down the centuries. Grumpiness is universal.

Maybe you don't vent like this—you just stew. A leaking, low-level irritability is a great temptation on a journey of love. You feel you have the right to be moody—you've earned it. It is a way of exacting emotional payment from a disappointing life. Grumpiness provides momentary relief, but it always involves a splitting of the self. I commit outwardly, with my hands, but not with my heart. I go through the motions of love, but anger smolders just below the surface like a simmering rant. Like Judas in his betrayal of Jesus, outwardly I'm kissing, but inwardly I'm betraying. The result? I'm split. My will has slipped off the tracks of quiet surrender to the Master, and I'm just going through the motions. Life ceases to be fun. If left unchecked, my inner moodiness begins to distort my heart, and I can slip into cynicism, which begins a downward trajectory into bitterness. It's not a good path.

Self-pity, compassion turned inward, drives this downward spiral. Instead of reflecting on the wounds of Christ, I nurse my own wounds. Self-as-victim is the great narrative of our age, capturing whole cultures. Jewish intellectual Peter Beinart, in his book *The Crisis of Zionism*, contends that the Jewish view of Israel-as-victim has blinded Israel to its treatment of Palestinians. Enshrining the victim is so seductive because you have been hurt. But self-pity is just another form of self-righteousness, and like all self-righteousness it isolates and elevates. It elevates you because it says you are better than the other person; you are the victim. It isolates you because you live in and are nourished by your interior world, which can't be criticized.

Here are five bad moves that our hearts can make when life isn't fair:

1. *Self-pity.* Nourishing an internal-feeling world of victim; compassion turned inward.
2. *Bitterness.* A simmering demand that God make my world just.
3. *Cynicism and mocking.* Restoring balance by mocking the other person.
4. *Gossip and slander.* Creating a community of empathizers who see my pain.
5. *Emotional revenge.* Withdrawing my heart to punish the other person.

All rob joy. In America, where we have incredible abundance, we are becoming increasingly cranky. Our touchiness is fed by an outlook on life that, following Emerson and Thoreau, enshrines the self. When feeling happy is the goal, we always end up testy because life conspires against us. Stephen Marche, reflecting on how our pursuit of happiness is leaving us exhausted, observes, "The more you try to be happy, the less happy you are."[8] But when love is the goal, we reap joy because no one can steal love.

The cure for a cranky soul begins by repenting, by realizing that my moodiness is a demand that my life have a certain shape. Surrendering to the life that my Father has given me always puts me under the shelter of his wings. That leaves me whole again, and surprisingly cheerful.

Submission, the Path to Personhood

Ruth responds to her mother-in-law's counsel with quiet obedience: "So she kept close to the young women of Boaz, gleaning until the end of the barley and wheat harvests. And she lived with her mother-in-law" (Ruth 2:23).

Lurking behind our allergy to submission is the fear that we'll disappear or lose our personhood. But for Ruth, submission is the path to personhood—not just submission to Naomi, but submission to her situation, to the life that God has given her, and to the humiliation that often comes with submission. Ruth has not sought the false shelter of independence. She is not afraid of disappearing because, in a sense, she's already disappeared—under the wings of the God of Israel (2:12). When you are hidden in God, you don't have to be afraid of being "under Naomi." Like Paul the apostle, who went from being "in Israel" to being "in Christ," Ruth has changed locations.

16

LOVE BURNS ITS PASSPORT

When Ruth mentions Boaz's name, Naomi sees the outlines of a resurrection: "Naomi also said to her, 'The man is a close relative of ours, one of our redeemers'" (Ruth 2:20).

Boaz, one of the family's "redeemers," has cared for Ruth. A redeemer, or *goel* (in Hebrew), was a male member of the clan who rescued another member, usually a woman, who had fallen on hard times.[1] One way a *goel* did this was by marrying the widow of his brother. Every male head of a family was a potential *goel*. A *goel* was a unique personalization of the law that provided not just rules but a person. What the US government does today with a dying bank a *goel* did with a dying family. A *goel* could restore property, purchase a relative out of slavery, avenge a relative's killing, assist in a lawsuit, and ensure that justice is served for a relative.[2]

A Redeemer Owns the Problem

The critical difference between what a *goel* does and how we normally help people is the level of ownership. It is relatively easy to give advice or tell people where they can get help, but a *goel* owns the problem.

I remember when one of Kim's social workers called all excited about something she'd discovered for Kim. She couldn't wait to show us. At our next meeting she brought a phone directory of our county's resources. That was kind, but it was not how a *goel* works. A *goel* picks up the phone, makes an appointment, and drives you there. A *goel* has a sustained ownership of the problem. A *goel* follows through, makes it happen, and manages through difficulties. A *goel* doesn't just write a check, but lets the weight of the problem come on him or her.

Jesus's parable of the good Samaritan provides a perfect picture of a *goel*. The weight of the beaten man's problems comes on the Samaritan. It affects his schedule (he stops), his provisions (he pours on oil and wine), his comfort (he lets him ride on his animal), his money (he pays the innkeeper), and his attention (he promises to return).

Recently, I watched Jill be a mini-*goel* with one of Kim's friends. Nancy had eaten large amounts of candy her whole life and not brushed her teeth in years, leaving her teeth completely rotten. Once when we took her to camp, her mother had packed her an entire duffel bag loaded with candy. Nancy was poor in every sense of the word. When Nancy's mom died, Jill stepped up her care for Nancy. Jill found a dentist who would replace her teeth for a small fee. Then came the ordeal of getting Nancy to the dentist, which included Nancy disappearing on the days of the appointment and lying. Jill dealt with Nancy's fears and dishonesty, drove her to the dentist, stayed with her at the dentist, and followed up. Jill owned the problem.

Redemption Is Messy

One of my first opportunities to be a *goel* came from my work as a deacon at New Life Church in Philadelphia. One of our deacons began to care for one of his neighbors, Paula. Paula moved closer to where Jill and I lived in Philly, and we befriended her.

Paula had five children, all by different fathers. The dads had disappeared from her life along with the three older kids. We started giving her money to supplement her welfare checks because they weren't enough to live on. She would call me in the evening to help her discipline her two boys. I'd run over to her apartment every couple of weeks and work with the boys.

Since I was principal of an inner-city Christian school, I began to think of how I could get her boys into the school. We had no extra money, so I hired her as the school janitor in exchange for tuition. Two days a week she drove with me down the Schuylkill Expressway in our station wagon loaded with eight kids to West Philly. I thought it would be a perfect way to help her with her work skills. I was soon overwhelmed.

Her works skills were awful. She'd come to work in slippers and a robe and shuffle around the hallways, lightly dusting the window sills. The place was filthy. She didn't know how to clean. In fact, she didn't know how to work. Her job experience consisted of selling hair-care products over the phone. Her boss had taught her to impersonate a big company by answering the phone in one accent as the "receptionist," holding the call briefly and then switching her accent to "sales," holding briefly again and switching her accent a final time for "shipping"! So, in addition to teaching full-time and being principal, I began to teach Paula to work. She was less than thrilled.

I soon realized that she needed a skill or she would be stuck in low-end jobs for the rest of her life. She thought she would like nursing, so we raised the funds and helped her get a two-year degree. She graduated as a licensed practical nurse and got her first decent job.

Not long after that, we discovered that she became engaged without any discussion with her close friends. Her fiancé was a resident alien from Nigeria, and I suspected that he was marrying her for the green card. Then I saw in her living room an inappropriate photo of the two of them. When I talked with her about the photo, she denied anything inappropriate, but it was hard to miss. After a year or two of marriage he disappeared.

After six years of "redeeming" Paula, I left the inner-city school and was less connected with her. When she got a job as an LPN, we stopped assisting her financially, and she switched churches. Frankly though, I was disgusted with her choices. A few years later she got cancer and passed away.

The story of Paula is no book of Ruth. What would I do differently? Lots. I would spend more time caring for her soul, making sure she was being discipled, helping her to think through her life and reflect on the pattern of sexual relationships without covenant, of seeking immediate gratification. I didn't take seriously enough the grip on her life of a debauched culture that lived for feelings. I assumed her appreciation of our care meant repentance. It didn't. I helped her situation, but not her soul. But my biggest regret was that I didn't stay in touch with her sons. I had a great relationship with them, and with a little effort I could have played a stabilizing role in their lives. I dropped the ball on *hesed* love. Nothing is easier to start; nothing is harder to finish than *hesed* love. Redemption is messy. This redeemer was flawed.

What went well? I was in Paula's life. She cost me time, energy, and wisdom. You don't just give money; you give your life, your attention. *Goels* practice *hesed*. They hang in there through thick and thin.

Top-Down Love

Toward the end of my working with Paula, my father and I started an overseas mission together. Our first team was working in western Uganda. I visited our missionaries there in 1986, and they took me over the Ruwenzori Mountains to some of the remotest and poorest tribes in Africa.

One of these tribes was the Babwisi. The team described their desire to relocate beyond the mountains and the enormous outlay of resources that would entail. While camping among the Babwisi in the western mountains, I thought, "I can endure in love for these people. They will not know who I am, but I can remember them. I can bear their burdens." I quietly covenanted with God and bound myself to them. For the next ten years, I recruited teams, raised funds, and planned strategy. That included a team leader, two doctors, an engineer, and several church planters. Some of them have been there twenty years now.

The redemptions of Paula and the Babwisi required attention, hard work, and persistence. But I loved them from above. Likewise, Boaz's love for Ruth is from above. It is the only way he *can* love her because he is above her. What makes Ruth's redeeming so extraordinary is that, like Jesus, she enters into the world of Naomi. That's what stuns Boaz. Ruth has burned her passport. She anticipates the incarnation, in which God binds himself to us in love, becoming a man forever. That is the essence of love.

The story is told of a missionary in Southeast Asia who was struggling to translate the word *love*. He thought the word was *pa* but he hesitated. It didn't seem to capture the word *love*. Then one day as he was crossing a swollen river on a makeshift ferry with several native women, they were all swept into the currents. He risked his life to save theirs. The natives told him as he was drying out on the river bank, "That was *che*

[love] because you were in there with them." With *pa* he was safe, helping from the outside. With *che* he was at risk, helping from the inside. That's *hesed* love.

If your risk is low, then you are a donor. That is wonderful. Every Christian is to be a donor, a giver. Just be careful. When you are simply a donor, advice and prayer can come quickly: "You need to get counseling" or "We'll pray for you." Redeemers own the problem; the weight of the other person's life falls on them.

So, in summary, we can describe three levels of helping:

1. *Donors* love from a distance. They give to help someone else, at little risk.
2. *Redeemers* (Boaz and me) love from above. They give but also do *hesed* love. They bind themselves to the person they love, at greater risk.
3. *Incarnation-redeemers* (Ruth and Jesus) love from the inside. They give their lives, at complete risk.

As far as we know, a *goel* or redeemer was unique to Israel. A *goel* looks forward to Jesus, the personification of the law who redeemed his people. As Jesus went around Israel healing the sick, caring for the poor, and including the outsider, he was being the *goel* that Israel never was. He completed Israel. When Jesus died on the cross, he was the *goel* for the world. God didn't simply send us a book of instructions; he sent his Son. He didn't just give us advice; he gave his own flesh. He didn't just show us how to do it, but he did it himself—all the way to his death. Jesus is the perfect *goel*.

I grieve that the church of Jesus Christ does not have more *goels* in it. To be a follower of Jesus is to be a *goel*. Scholars have generally focused on the Greek background to the New Testament word for *redeemer*, but *redeemer* is a uniquely Hebrew reality deeply etched in the Hebrew mind. Of the fifty usages of the word for *redeemer* in the Old Testament, eighteen refer to God redeeming and thirty-two refer to our redeeming one another. We've isolated the word *redeemer* to Jesus's salvation of us. We correctly think of the spiritual meaning of *redeemer*, but we neglect the need for everyday redeeming that is crying out all around us. Our lives should reflect the redeeming life of Jesus. If that were to happen, we would live not one life, but a thousand lives.

Part Three

LEARNING TO THINK IN LOVE

THINKING IN LOVE

The spring harvest passes quietly, giving Naomi time to think and plan for a possible marriage of her daughter-in-law to Boaz. But Ruth has no father or brother to act as intermediary. How might Naomi create a situation where Ruth can make a strong and effective yet private appeal for marriage in a village where everyone knows everyone else's business? To make matters worse, because of his prominence, Boaz is always surrounded by people. Ruth also needs a clear exit strategy so that if Boaz rejects the proposal, then neither Boaz nor Ruth will be shamed.

Despite the obstacles, Naomi comes up with a plan and shares it with Ruth, likely in the privacy of her home. Picture the scene: In the soft yellow light of an oil lamp, we can just make out the contours of a typical four-room Israelite home. Three long parallel rooms are divided by two rows of pillars with a fourth room for storage across the back wall.[1] The whole area isn't much larger than ten-by-twenty feet. One of the side rooms has a cobblestone floor where several goats and sheep are munching quietly. Against the side wall, stairs lead up to the second-floor sleeping area. In the corner huddled around a small cooking fire Naomi is talking to Ruth in hushed tones.

> Then Naomi her mother-in-law said to her, "My daughter, should I not seek rest for you, that it may be well with you? Is not Boaz our relative, with whose young women you were? See, he is winnowing barley tonight at the threshing floor. Wash therefore and anoint yourself, and put on your cloak and go down to the threshing floor, but do not make yourself known to the man until he has finished eating and drinking. But when he lies down, observe the place where he lies. Then go and uncover his feet and lie down, and he will tell you what to do." And she replied, "All that you say I will do." (Ruth 3:1–5)

Naomi's goal, "should I not seek rest for you?" recalls her first blessing on Ruth and Orpah, when she wished them rest on the road from Moab. But Naomi doesn't wait for blessing to fall out of the sky. She answers her own prayer by doing *hesed* with Ruth. She wants Ruth to experience *shalom*, the blessing of a settled peace that includes husband, children, and security, and she has a plan to bring that about.

What an audacious plan! To an outside observer there is no difference between what Ruth is doing and what a prostitute might do. As one scholar said, "What is one to think of a woman who bathes, puts on perfume, and then in the dark of night goes out to the field where the man is sleeping and uncovers his legs?"[2] If she is discovered, it won't look good. If one of my daughters had suggested this plan to me, I would have said, "Are you crazy?"

What could go wrong with Naomi's plan? Just about everything. Ruth might be seen. In the dark she might go to the wrong person. She might approach Boaz too early, when he hasn't fallen asleep and others might still be awake. And when she finally identifies herself to Boaz, he might take advantage of her or reject her.

A Neglected Aspect of Love

Naomi's brilliant multipart plan minimizes all those problems. By having Ruth go at dusk and approach Boaz only after he is asleep, she eliminates the possibility of Ruth being seen. By having Ruth observe carefully where Boaz lies down, she avoids the problem of going to the wrong person. By letting him sleep, Naomi reduces the risk that others would hear their conversation. By telling Ruth to curl at his feet, she reduces the risk that he would not notice her. And finally, Naomi counts on Boaz's character to not abuse Ruth.

The only remaining problem is that Boaz might turn down Ruth's offer. But Naomi's plan reduces that risk by having Ruth appeal personally to Boaz when he is in his best mood. If Boaz rejects the proposal, the cover of darkness allows it to end discreetly. But Naomi is confident that wouldn't happen: "He will tell you what to do."

Waiting till the end of harvest to reveal her plan also makes a lot of sense. Naomi has time to get her bearings and reestablish herself in the community. The timing allows Boaz to see Ruth's reputation grow, and makes space for love to grow. Waiting heightens desire. To propose immediately would be too presumptuous, too forward. Wisdom is sensitive to the trajectories of life. The sowing and reaping cycle can't be rushed. If we rush it, if someone gets promoted too quickly, if we get rich too quickly, if we get married too quickly, things can deteriorate in the long run. If you try to combine too many new things, one thing can muck up the other. For example, if Boaz says no, Ruth might be uncomfortable staying in his fields, which would hurt Ruth and Naomi's food supply. Naomi mercifully doesn't leave Ruth any time for worrying. If I were Ruth, I'd be thankful for not knowing because panic would set in if I had time to think about how crazy Naomi's plan is!

A neglected aspect of love is on display here—wisdom. Our culture puts "falling in love" front and center but forgets about "thinking in love." Not Naomi. She thinks about how to make love happen. That's wisdom. Without wisdom, Naomi and Ruth's situation would remain frozen.

Because we moderns have surrendered love to the world of feelings, we often separate thinking and planning from love. Our hyper-judgmental culture is quick to call a plan like Naomi's "manipulation," but that is only because romanticism hijacked the word *love*. When buying a home or starting a business, we present a plan to the bank or investors. They want to make sure that we've thought about everything. It is not manipulation to want to buy a house or start a business. So why would marriage be any different?

The Sexual Tension of Romance

Naomi tells Ruth to go to the *threshing floor*, *uncover* Boaz's *feet*, and *lie down*. He will *know* what to do. In Hebrew:

- *feet* can be a euphemism for the male sexual organ;
- *uncover your nakedness* is a way of saying sexual intercourse;
- *lie down* is another metaphor for sexual intercourse;
- *threshing floors* are places where forbidden sex might happen;
- *know* can be a euphemism for sexual intercourse.

All these words with sexual connotations can make us nervous. But the Hebrews weren't prudes. In a Jewish wedding, after the ceremony the couple went into the bridal tent and had sex while the other guests celebrated around them. The Hebrew belief in a good creation meant that sex was not dirty. Hebrew culture, unlike Greek, did not separate the physical from the spiritual, making the physical bad and the spiritual good. Because of the imprint of Greek Neoplatonism (the physical is bad) on the early church, it is hard for us to put *holy* and *sex* in the same sentence.

The choice of words gives the scene a romantic feel, a "delicate sensuality."[3] It heightens the mood, even the sexual tension. When an engaged couple waits for the public commitment of *hesed* love, you can almost feel their desire for each other. They touch often and look into one another's eyes. You can sense the energy. I've recently discovered that when the bride first appears at a wedding and all eyes are on her, my wife is watching the groom's face, measuring his love, hunting for passion. Purity creates passion.

God uses sexual attractiveness to draw men and women together in *hesed* love. Sexual intimacy reflects our image bearing, the divine intimacy of the Trinity. That's why Naomi pays attention to Ruth's personal appearance.[4] When I was discipling a young seminarian with a somewhat dour appearance who was longing for marriage, I encouraged her to take $1,000 out of her tithe and buy a whole new wardrobe. Twenty years later, when I had long forgotten my advice, she reminded me that it had worked. She'd gotten married!

Earlier Naomi and Boaz protected Ruth's purity. With this plan Naomi is protecting Ruth from loneliness. Our culture does exactly the opposite. By not protecting purity, it creates lonely lives.

The magic of sexual attraction in the book of Ruth is set in a framework of wisdom and purity. In contrast, the Disney paradigm of "falling in love" is invested with almost supernatural powers. No need for thinking or having a real relationship. So in *Cinderella*, the prince and Cinderella talk for only about ten seconds prior to their marriage. In *Sleeping Beauty*, the prince talks with Princess Aurora for about thirty seconds. Not a lot of thinking going on!

Love Risks

Ruth sets the plan in motion. Not only is the plan audacious, but so is the request. Ruth is a Moabite; Boaz is an Israelite. She is a woman propositioning a man; a servant asking a landowner; a poor person entreating a wealthy one; a young woman approaching a middle-aged man. Yet Ruth, with her trademark submission and spunk, follows Naomi's plan *almost* to the letter:

> So she went down to the threshing floor and did just as her mother-in-law had commanded her. And when Boaz had eaten and drunk, and his heart was merry, he went to lie down at the end of the heap of grain. Then she came softly and uncovered his feet and lay down. (Ruth 3:6–7)

Ruth bathes, anoints herself, puts on a cloak, and goes at dusk to the winnowing floor. (In winnowing, the chaff or husk is separated from the kernel by tossing the grain in the air on a windy day or by using fans, causing the lighter chaff to fly away and the heavier kernels to fall.) Harvest is a merry, party time, so Boaz likely stays up with his workers, talking, laughing, and telling stories. Another brilliant touch of Naomi is that Ruth will be approaching Boaz when his "heart [is] merry." The laughter slowly dies down as the harvesters curl up and go to sleep. When the last oil lamp is dimmed, Boaz makes his way to the edge of the grain pile and lies down, wrapping his cloak around him. When Ruth is sure everyone is asleep, she slowly lifts her head, checks her surroundings, hesitates, and then tiptoes softly to where Boaz is sleeping. She lifts up his cloak and tucks herself at his feet and waits. One audacious lady. She is all guts.

Three hours pass, then, Boaz stirs:

> Now about midnight, the man shivered, rolled over, and—lo and behold!—a woman was lying at his feet. "Who are you?" he said. "I am your maidservant, Ruth," she said. "Spread the corner of your garment over your maidservant since you are a kinsman-redeemer."[5]

By calling Boaz and Ruth a "man" and a "woman," the narrator lets us experience the confusion and ambiguity Boaz must feel. All we see is a man and a woman together. Emphasizing their gender further heightens the sexual tension.

Naomi isn't the only person thinking. Ruth makes sure her intentions are crystal clear. "Spread the corner of your garment" is a request for marriage that means to spread the hem of a man's garment over his future wife.[6]

So Ruth's actions (putting herself under the corner of Boaz's garment) match her words ("spread your wings") in the same way that her *hesed* commitment to Naomi was matched by her life.[7] Ruth is pure integrity.

Boaz blessed Ruth when he first met her, observing that she had sought shelter under the wings of God; now Ruth asks Boaz to be those wings. In effect, she is asking him to answer his own prayer of blessing! Through Boaz, God is covering Ruth under his wings. God works through Naomi's risky plan, Ruth's audacious obedience, and Boaz's love. One scholar summarizes it this way: "The reversal of the death . . . that [has] afflicted Naomi's life is effected by [God] through their ordinary hopes, intentions, and actions. . . . God often effects his purposes in the world through the ordinary motivations and events of his people—ordinary people like . . . you and me."[8] There is not a hint of passivity in the three main characters. God's sovereignty doesn't freeze them; it gives them the courage to be daring.

Ruth doesn't *exactly* follow Naomi's plan. Naomi told her to wait for Boaz after he discovers her: "He will tell you what to do." By speaking immediately, Ruth removes any possibility that Boaz misunderstand her intent. Furthermore, Naomi was just trying to find a husband for Ruth, but Ruth is asking for more than marriage. By calling Boaz to be a redeemer—to bear a child that would be Naomi's heir—Ruth is still making her own needs secondary to Naomi's. Her love is irrepressible.

There's more. Ruth doesn't request Boaz's help; she commands it. She doesn't say "would you please," but tells him, "Spread your wings over your servant, for you are a redeemer." Ruth prepares Boaz for the boldness of her request in the word she chooses for *servant* when she says, "I am Ruth, your servant." When she first met Boaz, she called herself a *shipkhah* or "lower-level servant." This time she uses the word *amah* or "handmaid," which is someone who is eligible for marriage. Ruth emphasizes the word by repeating it twice in her request to Boaz.

Thinking, planning, and problem solving are completely intertwined with romance, love, and audacity. Life is like this. When we separate love from thinking, love just gets weird and floaty, and finally tragic as lives are destroyed, all under the banner of "falling in love." It's good to think in love even as you are falling in love.

RIGHTLY ORDERED LOVE

We left Ruth at midnight and curled up at the feet of the most powerful man in town. She has just asked him, in fact ordered him, to marry her and thereby "redeem" her mother-in-law. You don't get more vulnerable than Ruth is at this moment. She has just shoved all her chips onto the center of the table. Boaz breaks the tension: "And he said, 'May you be blessed by the Lord, my daughter. You have made this last kindness greater than the first in that you have not gone after young men, whether poor or rich'" (Ruth 3:10).

Can you feel Boaz's passion? He's in love! He's fallen head over heels for Ruth. He honors her by calling her "daughter." He cares for her emotionally by blessing her, asking that the energy of God would come into her life. His tenderness, in the words of Cynthia Ozick, has "enchanted the centuries—a tenderness sweetly discriminating, morally meticulous, wide-hearted and ripe."[1]

Then Boaz commends her: "You have made this last kindness greater than the first." The word "kindness" is actually *hesed*. A fair translation is, "This time, Ruth, you have outdone yourself!"[2] When he says, "You have not gone after young men, whether poor or rich," he is suggesting that Ruth has put love for Naomi ahead of pursuit of beauty and strength, or status and wealth. He implies that Ruth has chosen him even though she could have the pick of the litter. Because her affections have been shaped by her *hesed* of Naomi, Ruth is not a perfectionist hunting for the perfect husband.

"And now, my daughter, do not fear. I will do for you all that you ask, for all my fellow townsmen know that you are a worthy woman" (3:11). Boaz continues to care for her emotionally by allaying her fears. Then he becomes her servant: "I will do for you all that you ask," in effect, reversing their roles. Naomi told Ruth to do all that Boaz would tell her, but here Boaz tells Ruth he will do all that she has asked![3]

Finally he explains his motive: "for all my fellow townsmen know that you are a worthy woman." Bottom line: "Ruth, everyone knows you are a gem." The ever-alert Boaz has heard all the good gossip from literally "the people of the gate." In other words, all the movers and shakers have been talking about Ruth. The medieval saying "a village is never wrong" means that the cumulative impact of your life is always known to your community. Let's listen in to their comments about Ruth as she passes through the gate:

- "Did you see how early she gets up in the morning?"
- "And did you see how late she gets in at night?"
- "I still can't believe she walked away from her country to live with Naomi."
- "Have you seen the difference in Naomi these last couple of months, with Ruth helping her? She's back to her old self again. I saw her laughing."
- "Ruth is attractive, but I've not seen her flirting with any of the guys. She stays really close to the women. Someone ought to fix her up."
- "She's a real catch."

Ruth "did not gain this reputation by trying to be somebody, by associating with the important people. On the contrary, it was her . . . *hesed*, her kindness and loyalty to . . . her mother-in-law, that has won her the praise of all."[4]

Boaz gives Ruth the same title, "worthy woman," that the narrator gave him earlier, "worthy man."[5] Boaz neither stoops to marry Ruth nor raises her to his status—he recognizes that she already has a status equal to him. The phrase "worthy woman" appears only one other place in Scripture, in Proverbs 31, which extols the virtues of a worthy woman. In fact, prior to Jesus, the most common placement of the book of Ruth in the Bible was after Proverbs. In other words, Ruth is a living illustration of the worthy woman. No other woman in the Bible is given that status. Only Ruth.[6]

A Love Rightly Ordered

All the barriers that separate Ruth and Boaz are torn down by what unites them: they both do *hesed*.[7] Boaz continues to care for Ruth by telling her not only his plan but also his problem:

And now it is true that I am a redeemer. Yet there is a redeemer nearer than I. Remain tonight, and in the morning, if he will redeem you, good; let him do it. But if he is not willing to redeem you, then, as the LORD lives, I will redeem you. Lie down until the morning. (Ruth 3:12–13)

Another redeemer has "first rights" to Naomi and her land. Notice that Boaz doesn't say, "Look, this is a marriage made in heaven. So no matter what happens, we're going to make this work." Any time self-will emerges—"I must have this"—an idol lurks underneath. An idol is always, to echo Augustine's phrase, a love out of balance or a love not rightly ordered.[8] The right order is God at the center and our lesser loves in submission. That frees Boaz to raise the possibility that this marriage might not happen. Even though Boaz is "in love," he doesn't idolize love. He doesn't let his love for Ruth run over the rules.

By respecting the deep structure of life, the covenants and relationships within which he is embedded, Boaz submits to God. Here are Boaz's two possible trajectories:

Idolatry. Ruth at the center ⇨ self-will: "I must have Ruth now."

True worship. God at the center ⇨ dependence: waiting on God to provide

What we worship, what we love, provides the energy and focus for our life, which in turn shapes our will. Jonathan Edwards summarized it best: our passions shape our will.[9] So if I were a car, the engine would be my passions, the worship center, and my will would be the steering.

When the well-dressed woman came to me at the end of our seminar saying, "My hands are bloodied from pounding on heaven's door," I sensed self-will. Her lament had become a demand. So when I invited her to die, to join "the fellowship of sharing his sufferings" (Phil. 3:10, NIV), I was inviting her to replace the idol of marriage with God. He brooks no rivals. He is, after all, a jealous God. Liberalism with its pathetic Santa Claus view of God abhors a jealous God. It prefers a carefree and tolerant God—a God of feelings with no power or resolve to back them up. But to be a lover is to be jealous of intruding lovers. A lover who isn't protective of his or her love is just a player.

Sexual impurity has a similar trajectory. Sexual intimacy outside of marriage is fed by an idolatry that puts pleasure before the commitments of covenant. It breaks God's speed limit by demanding immediate gratification. When that happens, love becomes disordered.

Coming Full Circle

When Boaz tells Ruth to "lie down until morning," he deliberately uses a nonsexual word, which simply means "lodge." Even though the atmosphere is sexually and romantically charged, the narrator makes it clear that Boaz and Ruth are chaste. The Hebrew word for *lodge* is the same word Ruth used when she told Naomi, "Where you *stay*, I will *stay*." Boaz takes the words of Ruth's commitment and transforms them into blessing. Her words of dying love come back to her as words of resurrection. The narrator, by using this verbal linking, reminds us that life is lived in trajectories of obedience and blessing, of faithfulness and hope. If God is guiding the pilgrimage, that gives us the hope to endure in love.

Finally, just as Ruth sealed her commitment to Naomi with an oath, Boaz seals his commitment with an oath. Boaz doesn't want to leave any doubt that the entire energy of his life is devoted to this new love. Just because he does not make Ruth into an idol does not mean that he is without passion. In fact, as C. S. Lewis says, when our loves are rightly ordered, our lesser loves come alive:

> When I have learnt to love God better than my earthly dearest, I shall love my earthly dearest better than I do now. In so far as I learn to love my earthly dearest at the expense of God and *instead* of God, I shall be moving towards the state in which I shall not love my earthly dearest at all. When first things are put first, second things are not suppressed but increased.[10]

Boaz's lesser love lay at his feet until morning. I doubt if they slept a wink.

Boaz Sends Ruth Off

> So she lay at his feet until the morning, but arose before one could recognize another. And he said, "Let it not be known that the woman came to the threshing floor." And he said, "Bring the garment you are wearing and hold it out." So she held it, and he measured out six measures of barley and put it on her. Then she went into the city. (Ruth 3:14–15)

Boaz cares for Ruth's reputation by using the cover of the early morning darkness to send her home. The gift of grain serves multiple purposes. It is a generous gift of food, heavy enough that Boaz has to lift it. It also provides cover. If Ruth is seen, it will just look like she is coming back from a long night of winnowing. The gift also symbolizes Boaz's commitment to redeem Ruth, a down payment on his love.[11] The seeds that will fill Ruth's stomach hint at the seed that will fill her womb and thus redeem her. That is more than speculation. Ancient Hebrew culture was well aware of the sexual pattern in nature. Boaz's love is not only rightly ordered, but overflowing.

DISCOVERING GOD ON THE JOURNEY OF LOVE

In the early morning hours, while it is still dark, Ruth makes her way home, laden with a huge sack of grain.

> And when she came to her mother-in-law, she said, "How did you fare, my daughter?" Then she told her all that the man had done for her, saying, "These six measures of barley he gave to me, for he said to me, 'You must not go back empty-handed to your mother-in-law.'" She replied, "Wait, my daughter, until you learn how the matter turns out, for the man will not rest but will settle the matter today." (Ruth 3:16–18)

We learn that Boaz told Ruth, "You must not go back *empty*-handed to your mother-in-law." The whole town had heard Naomi lament, "I left full but God brought me back *empty*." Because her grief was public, it sat on the community's soul. Two months later, Boaz uses the same word, "empty," reflecting back on her lament. He doesn't passively wait for God, but makes his own down payment on his determination to do her good. He wants to answer Naomi's lament, to overwhelm her with love. He wants to encourage her faith that a Good Shepherd leads her to green pastures and sets tables before her in the presence of her enemies. Now Naomi is on an upward side of the J-curve.

Boaz's gift of grain is pure poetry. He fills Naomi's metaphor of emptiness with grace. Because the ancient Hebrews lived in an integrated world of poetry and life, they were quick to see that metaphors are embedded in the structure of life. They saw the subtle artistry of a designer God. For example, Joseph took the metaphor of coats (he'd lost two) and silver (paid to make him a slave) and gave both silver and coats to his betrayer brothers. He transformed the metaphor of bitterness into forgiveness. The Hebrews didn't seize the day; they seized the metaphor that God was weaving in their lives.

What is Ruth to do? Nothing. Just rest. Naomi's reflection that "the man will not rest but will settle the matter today" is hardly even a prediction. "Not resting" and "finishing the job" describe everything Boaz does. Everything he does is prompt, thoughtful, observant, thorough, and determined.

Naomi's use of the phrase "not rest" brings us back to when Naomi blessed Ruth and Orpah, asking that God would give them rest. Ruth embraced her own blessing by, in the words of the foreman, "not resting" in the field while getting food for Naomi. Then Naomi answered her own prayer, saying, "My daughter, should I not seek rest for you?" In this passage Boaz "will not rest" so that Ruth can rest. Because of love, their lives have become interwoven poetry.

Discovering God's Design

The Hebrews were alert to poetic patterns in life because they knew their designer God crafted their lives. If you look carefully at your life, you'll begin to see designer touches too.

Let me explain by continuing the story I mentioned in chapter 3, the one in which Jill and (later) I yelled at our daughter Kim to get back in bed when she was pacing early in the morning. God usually involves me in the answer to my own prayers, and when I started to pray with Kim, here's what happened.

In late 2007, when I first went upstairs to pray with Kim, I was startled with a clear thought directed at my own heart: "You've underestimated Kim's ability to grow spiritually and thus own her own behavior." In the following year I couldn't get that divine nudge out of my mind. I began having devotions with Kim in the morning, but when it came to the prayer time, I multitasked by washing dishes. After my own devotions and taking care of Kim at breakfast, I just couldn't spare any more time. (I had to get to work and write a book on prayer!) The result was that Kim's prayers on her speech computer were perfunctory.

By the end of 2008, I finally stopped washing the dishes and sat with her while she prayed. Almost immediately, Kim's prayer life blossomed. She began to overflow with thanksgiving, thanking God for Disney, the latest movie she saw, or one of her crazy brothers who regularly teased her. (Last year on the eve of a trip to Disney, John told her, "Kim, they've closed Disney this year.") If her brothers were especially bad, she'd interrupt her prayer and "give them the fist." All through 2009 her prayer life blossomed. She began telling people she would pray for them, sometimes praying right then, putting her hands on them. Since she's had such a struggle with anger, she especially enjoyed praying for people who had problems with anger. Her prayers took a new turn when we lost our grandson Benjamin in 2009. She began to think more of heaven and whom she would see there.

The following year, while at Joni Camp, a camp for families affected by disability, Kim started complaining, almost freaking out, over pain in her elbow from an old break. We took her to the emergency room and the combination of her pain and a fear of hospitals caused her to have a complete meltdown when they were processing her. (Her meltdown did give us very fast service!) During the meltdown, she was furiously signing, "Jesus-help-me," forming the word *Jesus* by touching her middle finger to the palm of the opposite hand reflecting Christ's nail-pierced hands. When we got to an examination area, Kim quieted down. They took an X-ray of her elbow but found nothing.

About a week later, out of the blue, Kim typed out, "God spoke to me in the emergency room." I thought to myself, "Kim, we're Presbyterians; God doesn't speak to us." I'm half joking, but it is true that we are cautious of the language "God spoke to me" because it is so abused. So it is not something Kim hears. I was so surprised by her words that it was a couple of days before I asked her what God said to her. It was simple: "Don't be afraid. I am with you. Be like Daniel." This experience became a watershed for Kim.

Kim has her own business walking dogs, so she stops for lunch at our office. Recently, our office administrator, Dianne, noticed how Kim will begin to pray spontaneously during lunch. Kim has not been heavily influenced by the Enlightenment thinker Kant, so she doesn't know that you are supposed to separate prayer from the rest of your life. If someone mentions a need, she'll start praying in the middle of the conversation. She makes our lunchtime sparkle.

So where's the poetry? My sensitivity to God's voice ("you've underestimated Kim") opened a door to Kim hearing God's voice. When I prayed for Kim, she began to pray for others. I put my hands on her; now she has begun to do the same. I was praying for her patience, not realizing that I had similar struggles with impatience and multitasking.

God in the Shadows

The stories of Kim and of Ruth are perfect models of how God reveals himself. We discover him in our stories. We experience life, the story we inhabit, as if we are walking backward. The future is completely unknown. We see the present through our peripheral vision, through a kind of fog. Only the past has some clarity, and that clarity increases with time. "The characters [in Ruth] recognize Yahweh's actions only after . . . the fact."[1] When we reflect on the story we are in, we discover hidden there God's *hesed* love of us. That's what Naomi is slowly doing. God's love is becoming tangible. As we live a life of faithful love, as we are helpful in a cynical world, we discover the patterns of God's love.

But that is not our preference. We would like a little more clarity. Maybe a monthly Twitter feed from heaven or an occasional link to a heavenly YouTube video. In short, we would like God to be more obvious. But he stays hidden in the story. Otherwise he would be a cosmic genie, not a friend. A scholar explains how this works in the book of Ruth:

> Yahweh does not guide human affairs through intermittent miracles followed by long periods of apparent retreat. Rather, his activity is hidden behind the actions of human agents, yet he is presumed to be the implicit, immanent cause of events. Hence he is the cause of even the smallest "accidental" details of life. . . . One theological foundation on which the book of Ruth firmly rests is belief in God's hidden but continuous all-causality.[2]

God's presence in the book of Ruth mirrors his presence in our lives. It is subtle. He doesn't leap out like he did with Moses and the plagues in Egypt. If God regularly showed himself like he did at the Red Sea or the resurrection, there would be no room for relationship. Dramatic self-disclosure doesn't allow for the much deeper and richer form of knowledge of God's presence acquired as we do life in relationship with other believers.

By staying in the shadows, at the edge of the story, God creates the need for faith and thus intimacy. The hiddenness of God builds our faith muscles. It makes us work and think, like Boaz, Naomi, and Ruth. I had to work at my prayers with Kim. The result is that Kim and I both matured, learning to trust in God instead of our own strength.

We become different because God is subtle. The result? A divine community is formed. God is not a cosmic robot. He's a lover, drawing us in, wooing us to himself. We simply can't handle the full vision of God. Everyone in the Bible who saw it was overwhelmed (Isaiah 6, Revelation 1). The full vision of God sucks the air out of the building. We can't breathe. Emily Dickinson captures how God reveals himself:

> Tell all the Truth but tell it slant. . . .
> The Truth must dazzle gradually
> Or every man be blind—[3]

By keeping himself in the shadows, appearing at only the edges of life, God creates space for a real relationship with him. He doesn't overwhelm our vision, so we emerge and he emerges in our lives at the same time. We get to know God and ourselves simultaneously.

Learning to Live in the Shadows

To love means learning to live in the shadows, like Ruth. Not surprisingly, Jesus lived in the shadows. Even in the middle of a conversation, he often stayed deliberately small, at the edge, so others could emerge. His humility allowed others to come alive. Here's an overview of this pattern in Jesus's life:

- In Luke 7, when Jesus was at Simon's house and a sinful woman crashed the party, Jesus did nothing for several minutes while the women wept at his feet. The "space" that Jesus provided displayed her love and Simon's judging.
- In Matthew 15, Jesus deliberately remained at a distance from the Syrophoenician woman whose daughter was possessed by a demon. Into that space her faith emerged as Jesus gave her a faith workout.

- In John 8, when the woman caught in adultery was brought before Jesus, he created space by bending down and writing in the sand. In that brief interval the Pharisees' judging emerged. By waiting, Jesus created a situation that allowed him to speak to their hearts.
- In John 9, when Jesus saw a blind man, at first he quietly let the disciples react to the man. Their judging emerged, which in turn allowed Jesus to offer a whole new vision for this man and himself.
- In John 20, Jesus deliberately hid from his two favorite disciples and waited for Mary Magdalene. Even then he didn't reveal himself immediately to her. As a result, in her brief quest for Jesus, she emerged as a person. Then Jesus stepped from the shadows with one word, *Mary.*
- In Luke 24, on the road to Emmaus, Jesus hid his identity from two of his disciples. They discovered him only when their meal turned into a communion service.
- In John 21, at the Sea of Galilee, Jesus didn't identify himself to his disciples as he stood by the shore. They discovered him through his miracle of catching an abundance of fish.

In each of these incidents Jesus left "space." We don't feel space; instead we feel uncertainty and ambiguity, followed immediately by feeling forgotten and alone, which slips imperceptibly into despair and anxiety. The bad feelings we run from are actually the very place where love grows.

I remember when I first understood this aspect of Jesus. It was 1991, and I was beginning a sabbatical immersing myself in the Gospels. I realized that when John the Baptist was around Jesus, he wanted to disappear. "He must increase but I must decrease" (John 3:30). That scared me. I didn't want to disappear. I wanted to be known. Living in the shadows feels like death, but it is a death that produces life. Because there is less of you, there is more of Jesus in you.

In the words of B. B. Warfield, Jesus "did not cultivate self, even His divine self: He took no account of self. He was not led . . . into the recesses of His own soul to brood morbidly over His own needs . . . . He was led by His love for others into the world, to forget Himself in the needs of others, to sacrifice self once for all upon the altar of sympathy."[4]

When you love, you disappear. You are so caught up with the object of your love that you don't want to be seen. It is the opposite of pride. Scholars have puzzled over why the Gospel writers—Matthew, Mark, Luke, and John—are so hidden in their works. What these scholars don't understand is that when you hang around Jesus, you want to fade way because you are so captured by his beauty.

Ruth will now begin to quietly fade away. Her words to Naomi, "These six measures of barley he gave to me," are among the last words that she will speak in the story. She really gets love.

Love Leads to God's Unveiling

At every point, Ruth moves the story forward through her love. If she hadn't given up her life for Naomi, the town would not have discovered how amazing Ruth was. If she hadn't gotten up in the morning, exhausted from her journey, she would not have stumbled onto Boaz's field and met him. If she hadn't worked so hard in the field, Boaz wouldn't have been impressed by her.

It is critical for Ruth to keep obeying. Like a golden thread, her obedience weaves her pilgrimage into a stunning tapestry. When we step back and look at the whole, we see God everywhere—orchestrating, shaping, and redeeming. But without Ruth's obedience there would be no unveiling of God in the story. We discover God in the story as we love.

Obedience also drove the story of Kim learning to pray. Repentance was the trigger for obedience. My first repentance was going upstairs and praying with Kim instead of yelling. That opened the door to seeing that I'd underestimated Kim's ability to grow spiritually and own her own behavior. As I put feet on that repentance by having morning devotions with Kim, I was confronted with my multitasking impatience. One thread led to another.

We discover God through a steady obedience based on faith. Ruth's obedience opened the door to grace. Obedience didn't save her; it just put her on a grace-filled trajectory of sowing and reaping.

Faith and love work together in a kind of a dance. The Pauline formula "faith working through love" (Gal. 5:6) is the great discovery of the Reformation. Luther discovered that we must begin our Christian life, in fact, everything we do, with faith. To try to begin with your love is to begin with yourself, your power. That never works. But there is a secondary and neglected pattern in the Christian life, which Jesus describes just before his death: "Whoever has my commandments and keeps them, he it is who loves me. And he who loves me will be loved by my Father, and I will love him and manifest myself to him" (John 14:21).

Notice that Jesus describes our obedience as leading to intimacy with God or deeper faith. So the overall pattern looks like this:

Faith ⇨ love ⇨ deeper faith

What does this mean? Having begun with faith and constantly returning in faith to a foundation of God's love for us, we must move out in love. This looks like *hesed*, like Jesus's dying love for us. As we enter the life of Jesus (love), then we are drawn into a deeper fellowship with him (deeper faith). Then "my Father and I will love him and manifest myself to him." So the more we participate in the J-curve, the more we'll understand the depths of God's love. Love deepens faith.

Many Christians get stuck trying to grow their faith by growing their faith. They try to get closer to Jesus by getting closer to Jesus. Practically, that means they combine spiritual disciplines (the Word and prayer) with reflection on the love of God for them. But that will only get you so far. In fact it often leads to spiritual moodiness where you are constantly taking your pulse wondering how much you know the love of God for you. Or you go on an endless idol hunt trying to uncover ever deeper layers of sin. Oddly enough, this can lead to a concentration on the self, a kind of spiritual narcissism.

Ruth discovers God and his blessing as she obeys, as she submits to the life circumstances that God has given her. So instead of running from the really hard thing in your life, embrace it as a gift from God to draw you into his life.

Embracing the Really Hard Thing

Augustine's conversion is a parable of how we tend to avoid the really hard thing. When he became a Christian in the late fourth century, he put away the woman he'd been sleeping with for fourteen years, along with their son, and devoted himself to a life of chastity. For Augustine, conversion and chastity were inseparable. His heart had been so captured by sexual lust that he went cold turkey.

The woman he shared spiritual intimacy with was his mother,

Monica, who'd been praying for him for years. Later they shared to-gether a vision of the divine. There is real good in this: his conversion, his purity, and his mother's answered prayers. But Augustine, whose mind has done so much good in shaping the mind of the West, in this particular instance missed the application of the gospel to life. Under the influence of Neoplatonism, he shifted his quest for beauty from the physical to the spiritual. He didn't realize that lesser loves (such as commitment to his lover) are the door to the greater ones (God). Had Augustine married his lover (we don't even know her name) and loved their son, he would have joined Christ in his suffering and resurrection. Nevertheless, Augustine's later life when he was the head of a monas-tery reflected this dying love.[5]

The direct pursuit of the divine—the heavenly vision—hunts for an experience with God. But God doesn't like to be experienced. He wants to be known. We deepen our love of God not by direct pursuit of God, but through the good work of love, where we enter the gospel and the pattern of Christ's life becomes our pattern. Of course, we always have to begin with God's love for us—that's faith. But once we have that faith foundation, we deepen faith by love. That's what the J-curve is all about. As we enter a life of love, we get to know God.

Part Four

LOVE WINS
THE DAY

20

WISDOM IN THE PURSUIT
OF LOVE

During the long and likely sleepless night, Boaz figures out a plan to win Ruth. When the sun comes up, he is at the gate, ready to execute it. A typical gate complex had four rooms, two on each side, that would each comfortably sit twelve men. One side of the rooms was open to the traffic flowing in and out of the city. Whatever happened there would be known to all. That is where Boaz goes to work.

> Now Boaz had gone up to the gate and sat down there. And behold, the redeemer, of whom Boaz had spoken, came by. So Boaz said, "Turn aside, friend; sit down here." And he turned aside and sat down. And he took ten men of the elders of the city and said, "Sit down here." So they sat down. (Ruth 4:1–2)

As soon as Boaz sits down, "Behold, the redeemer . . . came by." The word "behold" suggests, again, that the hidden hand of God, not coincidence, is guiding events. Knowing God is in control emboldens us to plan. The way Boaz addresses the potential redeemer hints at his plan. Boaz says, "Turn aside, friend." However, the Hebrew word translated as *friend* actually means "so-and-so." Or as they say in Philly, where we have our own peculiar version of English, "Hey, Yo." The narrator deliberately makes the other redeemer nameless, faceless. It is a gentle jab, a hint that something is slightly off with this guy.

> Then he said to the redeemer, "Naomi, who has come back from the country of Moab, is selling the parcel of land that belonged to our relative Elimelech. So I thought I would tell you of it and say, 'Buy it in the presence of those sit-

ting here and in the presence of the elders of my people.' If you will redeem it, redeem it. But if you will not, tell me, that I may know, for there is no one besides you to redeem it, and I come after you." And he said, "I will redeem it." Then Boaz said, "The day you buy the field from the hand of Naomi, you also acquire Ruth the Moabite, the widow of the dead, in order to perpetuate the name of the dead in his inheritance." Then the redeemer said, "I cannot redeem it for myself, lest I impair my own inheritance. Take my right of redemption yourself, for I cannot redeem it." (4:3–6)

Boaz's demeanor here is strikingly different from how he was in past interactions. He comes across flat, almost passionless. In other business situations, all of which involved money or cost (new worker in the field, new worker at lunch, and a formal proposal from Ruth), he was passionate, even animated. We also know that he is eager to marry Ruth. So we wonder. Why is he so somber? Also, why doesn't he mention Ruth in the beginning? Why does he keep her hidden? Let's answer those questions by first examining Boaz's proposal:

- *First deal: Naomi only.* So-and-So buys Naomi's land and cares for an old woman for a few years. When she dies, the land is his free and clear.
- *Second deal: Naomi plus Ruth.* So-and-So buys Naomi's land and cares for an old woman for a few years. He also marries the young widow Ruth, supports her for the rest of her life, and supports her children, who get her dead husband's last name—not his. When those children are grown, So-and-So gives them the land.

Ruth's presence in the transaction dramatically changes the value of the land for So-and-So. In the first deal, So-and-So will increase the size of his estate with minimal loss. In the second, he will be throwing money away, thus endangering his estate.

Thoughtful Love

Like Naomi, Boaz uses wisdom to think about the best way to pursue love. He doesn't turn off his brain in his pursuit of love and goodness; in fact, he turns it on. Look how Boaz uses the principles of good negotiating:

1. *Let the other party name the first price, make the first move.* Most sellers will move off their stated price if you wait. Boaz lets So-and-So go first.

2. *Be willing to walk.* This is the hard part. Boaz has already told

Ruth he is willing to walk: "If he will redeem you, good; let him do it." Following the rules, conforming to the shape of life that God has put us in, is a check against idolatry, against demanding that God give us what we love. And if you are willing to walk, it puts you in a strong position.

3. *Know your opponent.* Boaz has his opponent figured out. He suspects that So-and-So is greedy and impulsive, and that he does not know or care about Ruth.[1] Look at the contrast between the two men. In the first day of Naomi's arrival, Boaz knew the whole story of Ruth. Two months later the entire town is abuzz with Ruth's character. That is, everyone except So-and-So. He jumps at the chance to get some cheap land, not realizing that Ruth is connected to Naomi! This guy is as close to the village idiot as you can get.[2] He's like the character Jim Carrey plays in the movie *Dumb and Dumber*, who upon seeing a thirty-year-old newspaper framed on the wall says, "No way, we landed on the moon!"

4. *Play your cards close.* If you are buying a house, you shouldn't even put all your cards on the table with your realtor. Anything you tell your realtor can easily be shared with the seller. That explains why Boaz doesn't mention Ruth at first. When So-and-So says yes to the first offer, he almost certainly has agreed upon an actual price. That is important to know for understanding Boaz's brilliance. Once a number is out there in good-faith negotiations, it is virtually impossible to back down, especially in a public setting where another buyer is waiting in the wings with a better offer. You can drop out, but you can't lower your price.

Now So-and-So is locked into the higher price because the price is public. Boaz is assured that he can protect both Ruth and Naomi.[3] If Boaz had mentioned Ruth in the beginning, So-and-So might have agreed to a lower price and Boaz might have lost Ruth. Once So-and-So realized that Ruth was part of the transaction, he dropped it like a hot potato.

5. *Know your goal.* Even though money is the *language* of the transaction, Boaz's goal is not money, but to help Naomi and to marry Ruth. This negotiation is a win-win situation because Boaz and So-and-So both achieve their different goals. So-and-So's goal is preserving his capital. Boaz's goal is Ruth, spending his capital on an object of his love.

Jesus calls us to be lovers with our money, not merely stewards. Focusing exclusively on stewardship can unwittingly make the preservation of money central. We see this in Jesus's parable of the lost son. If the goal of the father was stewardship, he would never have thrown away his money on his wayward son. But because the father was a lover, he realized that his son was on a downward trajectory, simply waiting for the father's death so he could live it up. As a discerning lover, the father speeded his son on a downward trajectory by giving him half his wealth. He condensed his son's life, enabling him to reach brokenness more quickly. *Unless the son tasted the bitterness of reaping while the father was still alive, the son could not be saved.* So the father sowed love by giving his son half his wealth and then waiting patiently for a return on his investment. In the story of Ruth, So-and-So is a steward. Boaz is a lover.

Prudence Protects Love

Was Boaz dishonest in playing his cards so close? Not at all. When we were selling our last house, I asked our realtor if we needed to disclose that there was a meat factory across the street. He said, "No, that's notorious information. It is so obvious you don't need to mention it." That is, to anyone but the village idiot. Boaz is being prudent.

> A prudent man conceals knowledge,
>> but the heart of fools proclaims folly. (Prov. 12:23)

Now Boaz seals the deal in a formal announcement:

> Now this was the custom in former times in Israel concerning redeeming and exchanging: to confirm a transaction, the one drew off his sandal and gave it to the other, and this was the manner of attesting in Israel. So when the redeemer said to Boaz, "Buy it for yourself," he drew off his sandal. Then Boaz said to the elders and all the people, "You are witnesses this day that I have bought from the hand of Naomi all that belonged to Elimelech and all that belonged to Chilion and to Mahlon. Also Ruth the Moabite, the widow of Mahlon, I have bought to be my wife, to perpetuate the name of the dead in his inheritance, that the name of the dead may not be cut off from among his brothers and from the gate of his native place. You are witnesses this day." (Ruth 4:7–10)

Boaz is all man here. Solemn. Strong. Authoritative. Clear. Careful. The precision of his legal language—an example of prudence—removes any ambiguity that someone could exploit.

Prudence for the Greeks meant making the choice that benefited you the most. Practically, that meant letting your mind control your emotions.

That gave rise to Greek Stoicism's dislike of the emotions, which has imprinted the church. In contrast, prudence for the Hebrews meant, "How do I avoid danger in a world of evil as I move out to love and obey God?" Biblical prudence is caution in the midst of committed love.

Biblical prudence protects us from the twin dangers of naiveté and fear in our relationships. Naiveté is fed by how our culture values openness and vulnerability. You spill your guts to a close friend and the next thing you know, everyone knows what you said. So you pull back, hurt and cynical about the possibility of friendship. Yes, your friend shouldn't have told the world, but it would have been better to be prudent, more cautious in what you shared. Prudence, understood this way, keeps us from needless pain.

Prudence also protects us from fear, from shutting down. As our world slips back into paganism, the old pagan fears are reemerging. As people become less trustworthy, we instinctively try to reduce risk. Thus, the young man whose parents divorce pulls back, hesitant to commit to a relationship or to pursue a young woman. He reduces risk by shutting down. In contrast, Boaz, Naomi, and Ruth never shut down. They relentlessly move into harm's way, yet they are prudent, reflective of potential dangers and thus cautious. Prudence takes total depravity seriously.

Perfectionism, yet another aspect of ancient paganism reemerging in our culture, doesn't allow for messiness. It evaluates life against an impossible standard that ultimately freezes people from risking commitment. In short, people are fearful of failure, of messing up. Consequently, our culture has a critical spirit, relentlessly Monday-morning quarterbacking "what went wrong." Look at the potential messiness in Ruth's going to an unknown land, going out to a field alone, and sleeping at Boaz's feet. Prudence can unfreeze us from the danger of perfectionism by anticipating messiness and minimizing the risk. It doesn't shut down.

The return to paganism is our instinctive response to a world increasingly devoid of a robust faith in God. The human heart reverts to paganism when it doesn't feel safe, when it doesn't know that a loving and sovereign God is orchestrating the details of life. So-and-So, like Orpah, chooses the safe path. His unwillingness to do *hesed* makes him nameless. He does the logical thing, not the loving thing.

Because our modern world has made the *feeling of love* sacred, there is no room for wisdom or testing the relationship. Feelings trump everything. The mystical power of love is warrant for not only sleeping together before marriage but also leaving the relationship when the feeling is gone. If you are in love, you don't need to think. In contrast, prudence reduces the downside risk in an evil world. It seeks advice. It asks hard questions. It follows the rules.

Prudence shapes *how* Boaz loves Ruth. Because men have a problem with sexual lust, he cautions his male workers not to touch her. Because people have a problem with jealousy, he cautions his workers not to belittle her. Because people have a tendency to judge, he gives her a sack of grain as cover. The right caution frees us to love with abandon.

A Life of Radical Love

Nevertheless, prudence should be an addendum to love, not the center. When prudence takes center stage, then caution takes over. So-and-So embodies prudence without love, the ultimate bureaucrat. The narrator sends us a subtle message through So-and-So: "Don't waste your life. Live a life of radical love." Cynthia Ozick, a Jewish-American writer, describes So-and-So's inner workings perfectly:

> In this closer relative we have a sudden pale reminder of Orpah. Like Orpah, he has only the usual order of courage. He avoids risk, the unexpected, the lightning move into imagination. He thinks of what he has, not of what he might do. He is perfectly conventional and wants to stick with what is familiar. Then let him go in peace—he is too ordinary to be the husband of Ruth.[4]

During the stressful years of starting an inner-city Christian school and then an overseas mission, I had a friend who would occasionally tell me, "Try insurance." In other words, take pressure off yourself and your family and make some real money. My friend's challenge made me face squarely the cost of my calling. My answer was always, "I only have one shot at life, and I want to give it my best. I want it to count." I say this cautiously because selling insurance is a wonderful calling; I've had a tax business on the side for forty years, and I love the challenge of growing a business. But I've had this passion to prepare the bride—the church—for suffering, for the coming of the Lamb. It's a passion that haunts me. I can't get it off my mind. So like Boaz, I chose Ruth. I sold all I had and bought the field with a hidden treasure. Many of you have done the same.

21

LOVE CELEBRATES

Now the party hats come out and the village begins to celebrate. Having patiently waited and followed the obligations of covenant love, Boaz finally wins his bride. It is a public kiss, and the village loves every minute of it.

> Then all the people who were at the gate and the elders said, "We are witnesses. May the LORD make the woman, who is coming into your house, like Rachel and Leah, who together built up the house of Israel. May you act worthily in Ephrathah and be renowned in Bethlehem, and may your house be like the house of Perez, whom Tamar bore to Judah, because of the offspring that the LORD will give you by this young woman." (Ruth 4:11–12)

Notice how the narrator deftly sketches this scene, letting the audience gradually grow. First it is just Boaz, then So-and-So, then ten elders, and finally the whole village. The villagers' blessing recalls the founding story of Israel (Rachel and Leah) and the founding story of their tribe of Judah (Tamar and Perez).

Redefining Feminine

The reference to Tamar is fascinating. Tamar was the daughter-in-law of Judah, likely a Canaanite.[1] When her husband, Judah's eldest son, died, Judah gave Tamar to his next son to fulfill the levirate obligations to Tamar. But Judah's second son didn't want to bear children by Tamar because the children wouldn't be his, so during intercourse he spilled his semen on the ground. That son also died, and Judah promised that when his third son grew up, Tamar could marry him. But when Judah's third son was grown, Judah didn't let Tamar marry him because he thought

Tamar was jinxed, even though God had slain Judah's first two sons because of their wickedness. Through no fault of her own, Tamar was stuck, childless and aging.

Tamar concocted a plan to force Judah to do the right thing. She dressed up as a prostitute, and when Judah was away tending sheep, she had sex with him, keeping his staff and signet ring as collateral until he could pay her. In effect, Judah gave her all his credit cards. When Judah's friend returned with the payment, Tamar was gone.

When word got out in Judah's village that Tamar was pregnant, he ordered her to be burned. On the way to her death, she produced Judah's staff and signet ring, saying before the whole village, "I am pregnant by the man who gave these to me." Judah was trapped, convicted of not providing a levirate marriage to Tamar. He repented to the whole village. He was wrong, not Tamar. She had twins, one of whom, Perez, became head of the leading family in Judah and Boaz's ancestor.

Both Tamar and Ruth are childless widows and foreigners who find themselves alone and vulnerable. Both should be redeemed but need to take daring action to make that happen. They have both been hurt, but neither wallows in her victimhood. Each comes up with a daring plan that involves approaching an older man for marriage in an audacious setting.[2] The result? These two feisty women become the heads of dynasties, even legends. No wonder the villagers think of Tamar when they see Ruth!

These gutsy women help us redefine femininity. They give way to neither Victorian fainting nor feminism's touchiness. They give us a third way in which femininity is defined as humility joined with power, sensitivity with guts. If God can use Tamar's feistiness to make her the mother of the tribe of Judah, what will God do with Ruth's *hesed*?

Faces of Grace

The last time Ruth is mentioned in Scripture is in Matthew's genealogy of Jesus. She is one of four women mentioned: Tamar, Rahab, Ruth, and Bathsheba. It is an unusual selection. Matthew leaves out the stars (Eve, Sarah, Rebekah, Rachel, and Leah) and instead puts in these outsiders. All are foreigners; all have a sexual cloud over them: Tamar pretended to be a prostitute, Rahab was a prostitute, Ruth seemingly acted like a prostitute, and Bathsheba committed adultery. What a mess!

The sexual cloud over these women's lives helps Matthew prepare the way for Mary and the conception of Jesus.[3] Jesus himself will be despised over his unique birth. In the Talmud he is referred to as "the son of a Roman soldier." God delights to take despised things, like Ruth, and use them as trophies of his grace, to bring down the powerful and raise up the weak.

The women also share Ruth's audacity. Each of them encounters enormous obstacles in a male-dominated world and breaks through to success. They are all feisty, courageous women, helping us to redefine what is feminine. As outsiders, each of these women in her own unique way is a living tribute to grace. God loves to use despised and broken people as trophies of his grace. Jesus is honored to have these women in his legacy.

Love Blesses

The blessings just keep coming: "So Boaz took Ruth, and she became his wife. And he went in to her, and the LORD gave her conception, and she bore a son" (Ruth 4:13).

"He went in to her" is a discreet Hebrew metaphor for sexual intimacy. God steps out of the shadows ever so briefly: he "gave her conception." Once before, in the beginning of the story, we glimpsed God's direct intervention: when Naomi hears that "God has visited his people and given them food." This inclusion subtly underlines that God has been orchestrating every detail in between. The Hebrews are artists. An understated truth always shines brighter than an overstated one. Less is more.

When the baby is born, the village women gather to share Naomi's joy:

> Then the women said to Naomi, "Blessed be the LORD, who has not left you this day without a redeemer, and may his name be renowned in Israel! He shall be to you a restorer of life and a nourisher of your old age, for your daughter-in-law who loves you, who is more to you than seven sons, has given birth to him." (4:14–15)

When I was teaching seeJesus's Ruth study, at this point in the lesson, an African woman almost jumped out of her chair and said, "This happened to me in West Africa!" She described how during a civil war she had fled to a neighboring country and started a thrift store. One morning the women of her village, led by an older storyteller, came singing and dancing into her store, celebrating God's blessing on her life. In other words, this scene isn't a construct of the narrator, as many scholars assume, but a real village celebration.

The Chain of Love

In Ruth's last act of love she gives her son to Naomi: "Then Naomi took the child and laid him on her lap and became his nurse. And the women of the neighborhood gave him a name, saying, 'A son has been born to Naomi.' They named him Obed" (Ruth 4:16–17).

Naomi takes Obed in her arms and nurses him. To this day in Middle Eastern villages an older woman will nurse another woman's baby.[4] The village women name the baby Obed, "one who serves." Just by being born, Obed becomes a *goel*, a servant to Naomi. His life means she has life in her old age. Ruth's redeeming set up Boaz's redeeming, which in turn set up Obed's redeeming. The chain of love works.

The year before, Naomi was gripped by grief, lamenting that she was empty. Now, she overflows, silently glowing as she absorbs the women rejoicing over God's goodness to her. Then, life was so bitter that she took bitterness as a name. Now, the women are naming a son for her. Then, Ruth was in the shadows, a nonperson overlooked by her mother-in-law and unknown to the community. Now, this forgotten but feisty woman is the star of the show. Life has replaced death. It is a complete reversal, a resurrection! The circle of paganism is broken. We are not trapped by our suffering, but liberated by love.

THE LEGACY OF LOVE

Remember how the book of Ruth began with death words—*famine . . . and he died . . . his two sons died*—and how Naomi was *left without her two sons and husband*? The book of Ruth began with death. It ends with resurrection.

Look at all the life and hope words in the book's closing:

> So Boaz took Ruth, and she *became his wife*. And he *went in to her*, and the LORD *gave her conception*, and she *bore a son*. Then the women said to Naomi, "Blessed be the LORD, who *has not left you this day* without a *redeemer*, and may his name be *renowned* in Israel! He shall be to you a *restorer of life* and a *nourisher of your old age*, for your *daughter-in-law who loves you*, who is more to you than seven sons, has *given birth* to him." Then Naomi took the *child* and laid him on her lap and became his *nurse*. And the women of the neighborhood gave him a name, saying, "A *son* has been *born* to Naomi." They named him Obed. (Ruth 4:13–17)

When the women say that Obed will be a "restorer of life," the word translated "life" is *nefesh* or "soul." It is the same two words in Psalm 23:3: "He *restores* [or turns] my *soul*." God has "turned" Naomi's life around. The soul that waits on God is always returning, resting in him.

When we first learned that Naomi's husband's name, Elimelech, meant "God is king," it seemed to mock God. But now "the name Elimelech, though sadly ironic at first, in the end turns out to be almost prophetic: God is indeed King."[1] God ruled by quietly reversing Naomi's complaint against him, by redeeming her.

Naomi never receives an explanation for her tragedy.[2] As she remained faithful to God, as she did *hesed* in the story that he permitted in her life, God blessed her far more than she could ask or imagine. When

Ruth embraced "the fellowship of sharing in his sufferings, becoming like him in his death" (Phil. 3:10, NIV), Ruth and Naomi discovered resurrection.

Celebrating Ruth

Even though the book of Ruth is about Naomi—it is her story—the women praise Ruth. Her love, her faithfulness, brought redemption. A more accurate title for the book would be *The Story of Naomi: How the Extraordinary, Unstoppable Love of a Moabite Woman Not Only Redeemed a Family, but Taught a Nation to Love.* "More than anyone else in the history of Israel, Ruth embodies the fundamental principle of the nation's ethic: 'You should love your God with all your heart' (Deut 6:5) 'and your neighbor as yourself' (Lev 19:18). . . . Ironically, it is the stranger from Moab who shows the Israelites what this means."[3]

Strangely, evangelicals have been slow to see this. Boaz is usually characterized as the Christ figure. Boaz is the formal *goel*, but Ruth is the Christ figure, the one who dies so others may live. One scholar puts it this way: "Everything that Ruth has done from the first scene until now has led to the possibility of the birth of this child of hope. It is Ruth's faithfulness, kindness, loyalty to Naomi, in a word, Ruth's *hesed*, has led to this outcome."[4] The whole town gets this. They don't celebrate Boaz; they celebrate Ruth. They give Ruth a twelfth-century-BC Oscar when they tell Naomi that Ruth is better than seven sons. To have seven sons is the absolute height of blessing, seven representing the number of completeness and wholeness. There is no higher praise given anyone, let alone a woman, in the Hebrew Scriptures.

Notice that the women don't idolize Ruth in their praise of her. They praised God for restoring Naomi: "Blessed be the LORD, who has not left you this day without a redeemer." Obed is the climactic expression of the love of God for her. God not only did not abandon Naomi, but he bound himself to her in *hesed* love. Obed's existence proves that. Sometimes in a moment of doubt, I'll glance at our daughter Kim's speech computer. It's a tangible expression of God's *hesed* of Kim that transformed her world. Because God is the primary love, the women were free to enjoy a lesser love, Ruth, as God's gift. Their loves were rightly ordered.

Essayist Cynthia Ozick summarizes Ruth better than anyone else:

> The book of Ruth—wherein goodness grows out of goodness, and the extraordinary is found here, and here, and here—is sown in desertion, bereavement, barrenness, death, loss, displacement, destitution. What can sprout from such ash? Then Ruth sees into the nature of Covenant, and the life of the story streams in. Out of this stalk mercy and redemption unfold: flowers flood Ruth's feet . . . until the coming of the Messiah from the shoot of David, in the line of Ruth and Naomi.[5]

"The life of the story streams in" when we're attentive to the story that God is weaving. Good lovers are good watchers, in tune with what God is doing. Otherwise, you'll collapse under the weight of love. As John said, "Whoever lives in love lives in God, and God in him" (1 John 4:16, NIV).

Early in the book I told you about my friend Debbie, whose husband told her, "I'm not in love with you anymore," and went and lived with another woman. Debbie was absolutely heartbroken. She shared with me that "after the anger passed, the sadness was incredible." But Debbie was attentive to the story that God was weaving. She prayed for Robert all the time—when she woke up in the morning, during the day, any moment she could grab. Debbie, like a child, clung to the simplicity of Scripture. In the midst of sadness, impatience, and faithlessness she read and prayed Romans 12:12: "Be joyful in hope, patient in affliction, faithful in prayer." She prayed that God would bring Robert to the end of himself. God did.

Robert turned. His soul turned. It's still hard to believe. Out of the blue one day he called Debbie and asked to meet with her. When they met he said, "I made a mistake." He told her, "I just couldn't stand myself." That same week, he told his live-in girlfriend that he was going back to his wife. Two years after his divorce to Debbie became final, Debbie and Robert were remarried. Resurrection happens.

The Legacy of Love

We come now to the final surprise of the book: Ruth is the great-grandmother of Israel's greatest king, David!

> They named him Obed. He was the father of Jesse, the father of David.

> Now these are the generations of Perez: Perez fathered Hezron, Hezron fathered Ram, Ram fathered Amminadab, Amminadab fathered Nahshon, Nahshon fathered Salmon, Salmon fathered Boaz, Boaz fathered Obed, Obed fathered Jesse, and Jesse fathered David. (Ruth 4:17–22)

The narrator has one last artistic touch for us: this ending or epilogue is exactly seventy-one Hebrew words, the same as the beginning or prologue. The seventh and the tenth names in a Hebrew genealogy are usually the most important. Boaz is the seventh and David is the tenth. Ruth is the founder of the greatest dynasty of Israel. "Suddenly, the simple, clever human story of two struggling widows takes on a startling new dimension. It becomes a bright, radiant thread woven into the fabric of Israel's larger national history."[6]

When David was fleeing for his life, he sent his family to Moab. Ruth was possibly written during David's or Solomon's lifetime in order to dispel rumors that David was a Moabite and to show God's design in David's heritage.[7] "That the greatest king of Israel should trace his roots to a destitute widow, her Moabite daughter-in-law, and an aging bachelor from the humble town of Bethlehem is . . . a supreme divine accomplishment."[8] This biblical pattern of strength from weakness, glory from brokenness, was written long before another humble woman from the same insignificant town of Bethlehem was the head of another royal dynasty.

The cheering begins with Boaz standing by himself in the field. By the end of the day, he has drawn his workers into his enjoyment of Ruth. Two months later, at the end of the harvest, the village has quietly joined Boaz. A year later when the baby is born, all the village women, in awe of her love, celebrate the work of God in Ruth. The circle continues to widen when her great-grandson is crowned king of Israel. Then the spiritual leaders of Israel honor Ruth's *hesed* when they place Ruth in the Bible. Now millions of us stand in her greatest Son's shadow, entering into his *hesed* of us and extending a chain of *hesed* to the nations. Like Ruth, we want to quietly disappear as we turn our eyes on him.

LOVE IS FOREVER

Everything Ruth does—from walking through the gates ignored and un-thanked to giving her newborn son to Naomi—is a function of her love for Naomi. She risks her honor by lying at the feet of Boaz, alone and vulnerable, in order to restore Naomi's family line. By marrying an older man she almost assures herself that she will again be a widow. This com-plete absence of self reflects the mind of Christ. B. B. Warfield wrote this about Christ's self-giving:

> He did not cultivate self, even His divine self: He took no account of self. He was not led . . . into the recesses of His own soul to brood morbidly over His own needs . . . . He was led by His love for others into the world, to forget Himself in the needs of others, to sacrifice self once for all upon the altar of sympathy. Self-sacrifice brought Christ into the world. And self-sacrifice will lead us, His followers, not away from, but into the midst of men. Wherever men suffer, there will we be to comfort. Wherever men strive, there will we be to help. Wherever men fail, there will we be to uplift. Wherever men succeed, there will we be to rejoice. Self-sacrifice means not indifference to our times and our fellows: it means absorption in them. It means forgetfulness of self in others. It means entering into every man's hopes and fears, longings and despairs: it means manysidedness of spirit, multiform activity, multiplicity of sympathies. It means richness of development. It means not that we should live one life, but a thousand lives—binding ourselves to a thousand souls by the filaments of so loving a sympathy that their lives become ours.[1]

Warfield's vision of living "a thousand lives—binding ourselves to a thousand souls by the filaments of so loving a sympathy that their lives become ours" is a perfect description of the Christian life. Every need, every person, is an opportunity to live another life. It is wonderful to connect with friends, but by itself it can feed tribalism, where your identity comes from your group. We've seen repeatedly how the quest for a feeling of love leads to a fractured self, manipulating or posturing. As our culture lurches back to pagan tribalism, recreating the American high school on a broader scale, we must ask the Jesus questions, "Who's lonely? Who doesn't fit in? Whom can I love?" Instead of trying to join a community, we can create community. We really have only two choices in life: a divided self or a multiplied self. We can either splinter into a thousand selves or live a thousand lives.

I wondered why Warfield understood so much about love until I discovered that on his honeymoon, while waiting on a train platform, his wife was struck by lightning. She became an invalid for the rest of her life. Warfield learned how to love in the trenches. When I mentioned this to a friend, he said, "What's the point of living if that happens to your wife?" I said, "Don't worry. The further you get into love, the easier it becomes."

You simply can't beat love. You can't out-humble it. You can't suppress it, because you are always free to love no matter how someone treats you. If others are putting nails through your hands, you can forgive them. If someone is shouting curses at you, you can silently receive them. Love is irrepressible.

Faith and hope will one day pass away, but not love. Love is forever.

ACKNOWLEDGMENTS

I am thankful for the input from these Hebrew scholars and teachers: Tremper Longman (Westmont College), Libbie Groves (Westminster Theological Seminary), Doug Green (Westminster Seminary), and Fred Putnam (Cairn University). My friend David Powlison of the Christian Counseling and Educational Foundation is always a blessing. Three commentaries listed in the works cited, those by Robert Hubbard, Daniel Block, and Frederic Bush, were particularly helpful, and I'd encourage you to get them for further study.

I'm particularly grateful for Liz Heaney's thoughtful editing. This is the third book we've done together. Thank you, Liz! I'm also thankful for feedback from these readers: Dianne Baker, Drew Bennett, Julie Courtney, Lindy Davidson, Ellen Eckhardt, Jake Eckhardt, Richard Eckhardt, Jane French, Lynette Hull, Shirley Kenney, Laura McCaulley, Jill Miller, Rose Marie Miller, Nessa Parks, Steve Scruggs, Thom Skinner, Courtney Sneed, Glen Urquhart, Annie Wald, and Justin Wilson. Thank you also to Julie Courtney for editorial assistance and to Seth Guge for your work on the diagrams. The team at Crossway, led by Lane Dennis, has been wonderful: Justin Taylor, Randy Jahns, Amy Kruis, Janni Firestone, and Anthony Gosling. I'm particularly thankful for the careful copyediting by Thom Notaro.

These five audiences who went through the Ruth study in 2009 and 2010 were wonderful teachers as well: our family (John and Pam, Andrew and Natasha, Emily, Jill) on vacation; Trinity Presbyterian Church, Lakeland, Florida; Chelten Baptist Church, Dresher, Pennsylvania; Line Lexington Mennonite Church, Line Lexington, Pennsylvania; and the First Congregational Church Men's Retreat, Hamilton, Massachusetts.

NOTES

Introduction
1. Names have been changed in personal anecdotes to maintain confidentiality.
2. For example, the Hebrew word for righteousness, *tsedeq*, means "straight." It is often paired with "path" as in Ps. 23:2: "He leads me in paths of righteousness." This idea of righteousness as a path is so deeply imbedded in the Hebrew mind that Jesus said, "I am the way" (John 14:6). The early church's first name for itself was "The Way." Paul the apostle exhorted believers to "walk by the Spirit" (Gal. 5:16; cf. Rom. 8:4).

Chapter 1. Suffering: The Crucible for Love
1. There are several alternative meanings of *Moab*, but this is likely how the Israelites heard the name.
2. Num. 22:1–25:9; Deut. 23:3–6. See also P. M. Michele Daviau and Paul-Eugene Dion, "Moab Comes to Life," *Biblical Archaeology Review* 28, no. 1 (January/February 2002): 38–49, 63.
3. Diane Coutu, "Putting Leaders on the Couch: A Conversation with Manfred F. R. Kets de Vries," *Harvard Business Review* 82, no. 1 (2004): 64–71.
4. Douglas J. Green, "Ruth Lectures," class notes on the book of Ruth, a course taught at Westminster Theological Seminary (n.d.), 13–15.
5. First Chron. 2:19, 50–51 tells us that Caleb's second wife was Ephrath. Ephrath's son Hur was the father of Bethlehem.
6. Fred Putnam (personal correspondence with author, December 21, 2010), comments: "This underlies the stories of Abraham's dismissal of his concubines' sons (Genesis 25) and the request of the prodigal son. His older brother (and their father) had every right to expect that the brothers would remain together on their father's estate even after his death. It also underlies the statement in Psalm 133—the brothers are still together. These customs are well-attested in ANE legal documents, especially from Mesopotamia."
7. Green, "Ruth Lectures," 7.
8. Putnam (personal correspondence with author, December 21, 2010) writes: "So does this mean that their parents knew when they were born that they would die at a relatively young age? Does it mean that they were sickly babies, so their parents thought, 'Why waste a good name on someone who's probably going to die an infant? We do not know how and when children were given names that they used as adults. Were these adult names given at puberty or names given when a child was weaned (c. 2–4), which would have given everyone plenty of time to see his or her personality, temperament, and etc.? Were they always given at birth, as Benjamin, Perez, Zerach, and Obed? How often were they assigned before birth, as in the cases of Ishmael and Isaac? We are working with very little data."
9. Later on, when returning to Bethlehem Naomi hears her name Pleasant, and she responds to the meaning of the name.

Chapter 2. Love without an Exit Strategy
1. Robert Alter, *The Art of Biblical Narrative* (New York: Basic Books, 2011), 93.

Chapter 3. The Lost Art of Lament
1. "More bitter for me than you" is my translation. I made this translation in consultation with several Hebrew scholars. The ESV reads "exceedingly bitter to me for your sake."
2. Robert L. Hubbard Jr., *The Book of Ruth*, New International Commentary on the Old Testament (Grand Rapids: Eerdmans, 1988), 112.
3. Libbie Groves, Hebrew instructor at Westminster Theological Seminary, e-mail message to author, December 2009.
4. Hubbard, *Book of Ruth*, 113, sees only "bitter complaint cloaked with firm faith," but Daniel I. Block, *Judges, Ruth*, The New American Commentary (Nashville, TN: Broad-

man & Holman, 1999), 637–38, questions Hubbard: "Her faith is apparently not as mature or orthodox as some would think." Block references Phyllis Trible's observation of the ironic ambivalence in Naomi's speeches. Trible, *God and the Rhetoric of Sexuality* (Philadelphia: Fortress, 1978).

5. C. S. Lewis, *The Four Loves* (New York: Harcourt, Brace, 1988), 121.

Chapter 4. Love Is Not God

1. Abhijeet Roy, "Gandhi and His Legacy (or Is It a Legacy)," *Something about Gandhi*, accessed July 20, 2012, http://gandhianexperiment.blogspot.com/2006/01/gandhi-and-his -legacy-or-is-it-legacy.html. Augustine wrote, however, that sometimes the best way to love your enemy is to go to war with them.

2. Cynthia Ozick, *Metaphor and Memory* (New York: Vintage, 1991), 252, 254.

3. Scriptures bear witness to a twin pattern of strong women and female poets: the Song of Miriam (Exodus 15); Deborah's poem after the defeat of Sisera (Judges 5); Hannah's poem after Samuel's birth (1 Samuel 2); and Mary's Magnificat (Luke 1). In our modern era our lives are enriched by the work of Christian women poets such as Emily Dickinson, Christina Rossetti, Luci Shaw, and many others.

4. Scholars call that pairing a hendysis, in which the mention of two parts is actually a reference to the whole. See Fred Putnam, *A New Grammar of Biblical Hebrew* (Sheffield, UK: Sheffield Phoenix, 2010), 39.

5. Adele Berlin, "The Book of Ruth," *Biblical Archaeology Review*, www.bib-arch/online -exclusives/ruth-1.asp.

Chapter 5. Death: The Center of Love

1. Robert L. Hubbard Jr., *The Book of Ruth*, New International Commentary on the Old Testament (Grand Rapids: Eerdmans, 1988), 118, 120.

2. Katherine Doob Sakenfeld, *Interpretation: A Bible Commentary for Preaching and Teaching: Ruth* (Louisville, KY: John Knox, 1999), 33.

3. Of course God has *voluntarily* bound himself to us in love. I like the vividness of "God is trapped" because it highlights the binding quality of God's *hesed* love. The Christian God is bound by his love, unlike Allah, who is completely free and cannot commit himself to his followers.

4. This is not just a devotional insight. It bears the weight of the entire book. At every stage, Ruth is Naomi's redeemer par excellence. Boaz is the formal redeemer; Ruth is the de facto one. In chapter 2 Boaz tells Ruth how the whole village is stunned by her love. He shares that awe of her love. In chapter 4, the women's chorus celebrates Ruth's love, not Boaz's. Ruth is God's response to Naomi's grief.

5. Several commentators say that the Hebrew implies they walked in silence.

6. Fred Putnam, personal correspondence with author, December 21, 2010: "An Abraham-Ruth comparison is valid because there are numerous allusions to Genesis in *Ruth*. Patterns that *Ruth* picks up from Genesis: Ruth 2:11—Genesis 2:24, 12:1, 31:13; Ruth 1:1—Genesis 12:10, 26:1; Ruth 3:1–9—Genesis 19:30–38; Ruth 2:20—Genesis 24:27; . . . Ruth 4:18—parallel pattern in Genesis genealogies." See also Daniel I. Block, "Book of Ruth 1," in *Dictionary of the Old Testament: Wisdom, Poetry and Writings*, ed. Tremper Longman III and Peter Enns (Downers Grove, IL: IVP Academic, 2008), 680. See also Frederic W. Bush, *Ruth, Esther*, Word Biblical Commentary (Nashville, TN: Thomas Nelson, 1996), 128. One of the reasons for this is the statement "And there was a famine in the land" in Ruth 1:1 and Genesis 12:10 (the only two times that this clause occurs).

7. Phyllis Trible, "A Human Comedy," in *God and the Rhetoric of Sexuality* (Philadelphia: Fortress, 1978), 173. There is some overstatement in Trible's last sentence. Certainly, Ruth's faith is on par with Abraham's when he offers Isaac, David's when he confronts Goliath, and Daniel and his friends' when they confront Nebuchadnezzar.

Chapter 6. Entering a Broken Heart

1. This classic pattern of Israelite gates found at Hazor, Gezer, and Mediggo dates from the time of Solomon or a hundred years later. Gates like these have also been found in Moab.

2. Some cultures are very attuned to the meanings of names. I visited Kenya with a friend of

mine, Steve Smallman. Steve is a big man, over six feet. When the Kenyans met him, they all started laughing because he was not a small man. Growing up in the West, I'd never thought of the meaning of his name before.

3. We are not certain what "the Almighty" or *El Shaddai* means. Wikipedia has an excellent summary of the complex discussion of the meaning of *El Shaddai*, www.en.wikipedia .org/wiki/El_Shaddai.

4. Daniel I. Block, *Judges, Ruth*, The New American Commentary (Nashville, TN: Broadman & Holman, 1999), 647, "She does indeed ascribe sovereignty to God, but this is a sovereignty without grace, an omnipotent power without compassion, a judicial will without mercy." Older Christian interpretations have almost exclusively seen Naomi as bitter. More recent scholarship has reacted to this and swung in the opposite direction. I think the text drives us to see Naomi as struggling with bitterness, but not succumbing to it.

5. Tremper Longman III, personal correspondence with author, December 30, 2009.

6. C. S. Lewis, *The Screwtape Letters* (New York: HarperCollins, 1996), 40.

Chapter 7. Discovering Glory in Love

1. Robert Alter, *The Art of Biblical Narrative* (New York: Basic Books, 2011), 158, 144.

2. George Orwell, quoted by Benjamin Schwartz, "The Hitch," *The Atlantic*, March 2012, 78.

3. John Stott, *The Cross of Christ* (Downers Grove, IL: InterVarsity, 1986), 205.

Chapter 8. Loving against My Feelings

1. Ruth 1:6, "return"; 1:7, "return"; 1:8, "return"; 1:10, "return"; 1:11, "turn back"; 1:12, "turn back"; 1:15, "gone back," "return"; 1:16, "return"; 1:21, "brought me back"; 1:22, "returned," "returned."

2. Some scholars take exception to this and suggest that Elimelech is at fault. The text clearly mentions him taking his family out. Yet Naomi appears to be a full partner in leaving. When she laments in 1:21, "I went away full," there is no regret on her part, and she doesn't distance herself from Elimelech as Eve does from Adam.

3. Daniel I. Block, *Judges, Ruth*, The New American Commentary (Nashville, TN: Broadman & Holman, 1999), 613.

4. First Lot is pitching his tent near Sodom (Gen. 13:12), then Lot is living in Sodom (14:12).

5. G. K. Chesterton, *Orthodoxy* (New York: Doubleday, 1959), 53.

6. C. S. Lewis, *Surprised by Joy* (New York: Harcourt Brace Jovanovich, 1966), 229.

7. Stephen Marche, "Is Facebook Making Us Lonely?" *The Atlantic*, May 2012, 69–70.

Chapter 9. The Gospel Shape of Love

1. Michael Homan, "Did the Israelites Drink Beer?," *Biblical Archaeology Review* 36, no. 5 (September/October 2010): 48–56.

2. The Gezer calendar dates to the tenth century BC. It is one of our oldest Hebrew scripts. The author is Abijah (*Abi* = "my father," *jah* = *Yahweh*, meaning "my-Father-is-Yahweh"). The calendar reads:
   - Two months of harvest
   - Two months of planting
   - Two months of late planting
   - One month of hoeing
   - One month of barley harvest
   - One month of harvest and festival
   - Two months of grape harvesting
   - One month of summer fruit

3. Robert L. Hubbard Jr., *The Book of Ruth*, New International Commentary on the Old Testament (Grand Rapids: Eerdmans, 1988), 129.

4. Thomas Cahill, *Desire of the Everlasting Hills* (New York: Doubleday, 1999), 60–61.

5. Heraclitus, *Fragments: The Collected Wisdom of Heraclitus*, trans. Brooks Haxton (New York: Viking, 2001), 15, 45.

6. Cahill, *Desire of the Everlasting Hills*, 61.

7. George Orwell, quoted by Benjamin Schwartz, "The Hitch," *The Atlantic*, March 2012, 78.

8. Robert Alter, *The Art of Biblical Narrative* (New York: Basic Books, 2011), 27; see also 134. Alter is summarizing Herbert Schneidau's thesis in *Sacred Discontent*.
9. Douglas J. Green, "Ruth Lectures," class notes on the book of Ruth, a course taught at Westminster Theological Seminary (n.d.), 10.

Chapter 10. Love Lands

1. This is an argument from silence. We don't know for sure that Naomi's passivity reflects something wrong with her. I include this suggestion because several scholars mention it, and it does fit the overall pattern in Naomi's life at this point and the general pattern with people who are struggling with bitterness.
2. David Brooks, "It's Not About You," *New York Times*, May 30, 2011, sec. A, 23.
3. As quoted by Tim Keller, "Absolutism: Don't We All Have to Find Truth for Ourselves?," sermon delivered at Redeemer Presbyterian Church, New York, October 8, 2006.
4. This is an example of hyperbole, overstating a negative (or a positive) to show the opposite.
5. The division between men and women harvest teams that we'll see later in this chapter is reflected in Egyptian pictures of harvesting. "Ancient Egypt: The Grain Harvest," accessed March 2012, http://www.reshafim.org.il/ad/egypt/timelines/topics/harvesting_grain.htm.
6. Robert L. Hubbard Jr., *The Book of Ruth*, New International Commentary on the Old Testament (Grand Rapids: Eerdmans, 1988), 138.
7. Edges of fields were not defined by fences, so reapers might leave some at the edge so as not to encroach on their neighbor's field. Also there would be more weeds on the edges.
8. David Powlison, personal correspondence with author, July 31, 2012.

Chapter 11. Love Protects

1. Frederic W. Bush, *Ruth, Esther*, Word Biblical Commentary (Nashville, TN: Thomas Nelson, 1996), 113.
2. Douglas J. Green, "Ruth Lectures," class notes on the book of Ruth, a course taught at Westminster Theological Seminary (n.d.), 5.
3. Robert L. Hubbard Jr., *The Book of Ruth*, New International Commentary on the Old Testament (Grand Rapids: Eerdmans, 1988), 162.
4. Libbie Groves, personal correspondence with author, November 17, 2010.
5. A *short rest* is an educated guess. The Hebrew would be translated literally, "this her sitting (or dwelling) in the house a little." We don't know whether "little" is a time reference (short rest), or a size reference (short house or hut in the field for reapers), or a short time in the village in Naomi's home (she stayed only a short time with Naomi in her house before coming out); or whether it means of little importance (she's practically taken up residence in the field; the hut means little to her). Nor do we know whether "house" means home in the village or a shelter in the field. Hubbard, *Book of Ruth*, 151, makes a proposal, but Block and others discount his thesis. The Septuagint translation (250 BC, the oldest translation of the Old Testament) would yield this wording of v. 7: ". . . and she came and stood from morning til evening and rested not even a little in the field." Regardless, most of these possibilities suggest that Ruth is a hard worker.
6. Ibid., 155.
7. Libbie Groves, personal correspondence with author, November 17, 2010.
8. Boaz might be issuing the order loudly at this point for all to hear. See Hubbard, *Book of Ruth*, 158.
9. Tim Keller, "The Insider and the Outsider Encounter Jesus," lecture delivered at the Oxford Inter-Collegiate Christian Union, Oxford University, February 8, 2012. I have condensed Keller's longer answer to a question raised during a Q&A time.
10. Dietrich Bonhoeffer, *Letters and Papers from Prison* (New York: Touchstone, 1997), 43.
11. Kate Bolick, "All the Single Ladies," *The Atlantic*, November 2011, 124.
12. Meg Jay, "The Downside of Cohabiting before Marriage," *New York Times*, April 14, 2012, sec. SR, 4.
13. Kate Bolick, "All the Single Ladies," 124.
14. Ibid., 126.
15. Hubbard, *Book of Ruth*, 163.

16. Ibid., 157. See "Ayin," *Theologisches Handwörterbuch zum Alten Testament*, ed. E. Jenni, vol. 2 (Munich: Kaiser, 1976).

17. Matt. 9:36; Mark 6:34; 10:21; Luke 7:13; 10:33–35; 15:20; 19:5, 41; John 6:5; 11:33; 19:26 are just a few other examples. For a fuller treatment of this pattern in Jesus's life, see my book, *Love Walked among Us: Learning to Love Like Jesus* (Colorado Springs: NavPress, 2001).

Chapter 12. The World Moves for Love

1. Robert L. Hubbard Jr., *The Book of Ruth*, New International Commentary on the Old Testament (Grand Rapids: Eerdmans, 1988), 164.

2. Daniel I. Block, *Judges, Ruth*, The New American Commentary (Nashville, TN: Broadman & Holman, 1999), 661.

3. I am using the word *worship* the same way Shyamalan does—that is, a generic way of saying we are enthralled by someone or something. Of course, we worship God alone. But all of us engage in low-level worship with what Augustine calls our "lesser loves."

4. "Repay" is *shalam* in Hebrew.

5. Block, *Judges, Ruth*, 663; Hubbard, *Book of Ruth*, 165–66.

6. (1) Naomi blesses Ruth and Orpah (1:8–9). (2) Boaz blesses his workers (2:4). (3) Workers bless Boaz (2:4). (4) Boaz blesses Ruth (2:12). (5) Naomi blesses Boaz (2:19). (6) Naomi blesses Boaz (2:20). (7) Boaz blesses Ruth (3:10). (8) Elders bless Boaz (4:11–12). (9) Women bless the Lord (4:14). (10) Women bless Obed (4:14–15).

7. Hubbard, *Book of Ruth*, 70.

Chapter 13. Humility: The Path of Love

1. Robert L. Hubbard Jr., *The Book of Ruth*, New International Commentary on the Old Testament (Grand Rapids: Eerdmans, 1988), 171.

2. "Allayed my fears" is my translation. See Frederic W. Bush, *Ruth, Esther*, Word Biblical Commentary (Nashville, TN: Thomas Nelson, 1996), 124.

3. Hubbard, *Book of Ruth*, 169.

4. Daniel I. Block, *Judges, Ruth*, The New American Commentary (Nashville, TN: Broadman & Holman, 1999), 665.

5. Hubbard, *Book of Ruth*, 171.

6. Accessed August 16, 2012, http://www.astheworldsleeps.org/node/4910.

7. For a detailed examination of this theme in Jesus's life, see chapter 13 of Paul E. Miller, *Love Walked among Us: Learning to Love Like Jesus* (Colorado Springs: NavPress, 2001).

8. Notes from Dr. Steve Jamison, who lived in Egypt as a missionary.

9. Block, *Judges, Ruth*, 667.

10. Ibid., 659.

Chapter 14. Love Creates Community

1. I'm indebted to Courtney Sneed for this insight.

2. R. R. Reno, "Postmodern Irony and Petronian Humanism," Mars Hill Audio Resources Essay, vol. 67 (March/April 2004): 6–7.

3. Of the four main sects of first-century Judaism (Pharisees, Sadducees, Zealots, and Essenes), the Essenes have received the most scholarly attention of late. It appears that Qumran was a kind of Essene "university." No one is suggesting that Jesus is an Essene, but his teaching is in harmony with the Essene emphasis on community and poverty, and the Essenes are the only group of the first century that Jesus does not criticize. The Essenes had three community houses for travelers on the east side of Jerusalem. Bethany, the name of which means house of the poor, was one of them. This is where Mary, Martha, and Lazarus live, all singles, which is highly unusual outside of Essene culture. Judas at a dinner at Bethany, saying, "Why couldn't this have been given to the poor?," fits with these being Essene villages. Brian J. Capper, "Essene Community Houses and Jesus' Early Community," in *Jesus and Archaeology*, ed. James Charlesworth (Grand Rapids: Eerdmans, 2006), 472–502.

Chapter 15. Love Invites Resurrection

1. Robert L. Hubbard Jr., *The Book of Ruth*, New International Commentary on the Old Testament (Grand Rapids: Eerdmans, 1988), 179. If Ruth started at 6:00 a.m., worked in the fields until evening, then beat the grain and walked back to the city, Ruth would have walked in the door around 10:00 p.m. Because food costs would have been 90 percent of living costs, the ephah would have essentially covered her expenses for two weeks or more.
2. Daniel I. Block, *Judges, Ruth*, The New American Commentary (Nashville, TN: Broadman & Holman, 1999), 671. The repetitiveness of the questions and how they are jumbled together suggest her astonishment.
3. Frederic W. Bush, *Ruth, Esther*, Word Biblical Commentary (Nashville, TN: Thomas Nelson, 1996), 141.
4. Is Naomi referring to Boaz or the Lord in 2:20 when she says, "who has not abandoned his *hesed* to the living and the dead!" (my trans.)? Who is the person who has not abandoned his hesed? It could be Boaz or God. Libbie Groves (personal correspondence with author, November 17, 2010) comments, "There is a delightful ambiguity in the Hebrew in her response. It is ambiguous who is being referred to by the 'who has not . . . .' Is it Boaz who is showing *hesed*? Or it is the Lord? Possibly both as a way of showing that God is doing his *hesed* through Boaz."
5. Hubbard, *The Book of Ruth*, 187.
6. Donald Rauber, "Literary Values in the Bible: The Book of Ruth," *Journal of Biblical Literature* 89, no. 1 (1970): 32–33.
7. Robert Alter, *The Art of Biblical Narrative* (New York: Basic Books, 2011), 158.
8. Stephen Marche, "Is Facebook Making Us Lonely?," *The Atlantic*, May 2012, 69.

Chapter 16. Love Burns Its Passport

1. Daniel I. Block, *Judges, Ruth*, The New American Commentary (Nashville, TN: Broadman & Holman, 1999), 674.
2. Ibid.; see Lev. 25:25–30, 47–55; Num. 5:8; 35:12, 19–27; Job 19:25; Ps. 119:154; Jer. 50:34.

Chapter 17. Thinking in Love

1. Shlomo Bunimovitz and Avraham Faust, "Ideology in Stone: Understanding the Four-Room House," *Biblical Archaeology Review* 28, no. 4 (July/August 2002): 32–41.
2. Daniel I. Block, *Judges, Ruth*, The New American Commentary (Nashville, TN: Broadman & Holman, 1999), 686.
3. Robert L. Hubbard Jr., *The Book of Ruth*, New International Commentary on the Old Testament (Grand Rapids: Eerdmans, 1988), 209.
4. Some translations say "best dress," but the garment (*simlah*) that Ruth put on was just a cloak that could be used as a blanket. If an Israelite took a poor person's *simlah* as a security, he or she had to return it before nightfall so the owner wouldn't get cold (Ex. 22:26–27). The Bible's closest parallel to Naomi's instructions appears in 2 Sam. 12:20, when David learns of the death of his child: "He washed himself and put on perfumed oil and changed his *simlah*" (my trans.). When mourning, people refrained from washing themselves or anointing themselves with oil (2 Sam. 14:2). Most likely Naomi was telling Ruth to end her period of mourning for her husband.
5. Hubbard, *The Book of Ruth*, 207.
6. Frederic W. Bush, *Ruth, Esther*, Word Biblical Commentary (Nashville, TN: Thomas Nelson, 1996), 164. See Ezek. 16:8. "Spreading the garment" is still practiced in some Arab cultures today.
7. Ibid., 180.
8. Ibid., 55.

Chapter 18. Rightly Ordered Love

1. Cynthia Ozick, *Metaphor and Memory* (New York: Vantage, 1991), 261.
2. Robert L. Hubbard Jr., *The Book of Ruth*, New International Commentary on the Old Testament (Grand Rapids: Eerdmans, 1988), 207.

3. Daniel I. Block, *Judges, Ruth*, The New American Commentary (Nashville, TN: Broadman & Holman, 1999), 694.

4. Ibid., 694–95.

5. D. Ulrich, "Ruth 4: Person," in *Dictionary of the Old Testament: Wisdom, Poetry and Writings*, ed. Tremper Longman III and Peter Enns (Downers Grove, IL: IVP Academic, 2008), 702.

6. Daniel I. Block, "Book of Ruth 1," in Longman and Enns, *Dictionary of the Old Testament*, 683.

7. Frederic W. Bush, *Ruth, Esther*, Word Biblical Commentary (Nashville, TN: Thomas Nelson, 1996), 182.

8. Michael Austin, "Achieving Happiness: Advice from Augustine," accessed July 20, 2012, http://www.psychologytoday.com/blog/ethics-everyone/201106/achieving-happiness-advice -augustine.

9. George M. Marsden, *A Short Life of Jonathan Edwards* (Grand Rapids: Eerdmans, 2008), 78.

10. C. S. Lewis, *Letters of C. S. Lewis*, ed. W. H. Lewis (New York: Harcourt Brace Jovanovich, 1966), 248.

11. Bush, *Ruth, Esther*, 182.

Chapter 19. Discovering God on the Journey of Love

1. Robert L. Hubbard Jr., *The Book of Ruth*, New International Commentary on the Old Testament (Grand Rapids: Eerdmans, 1988), 72.

2. Ibid., 70.

3. Emily Dickinson, "Tell All the Truth, but Tell It Slant," accessed February 19, 2013, http://www.canopicpublishing.com/poets/dickinsonTruth.htm.

4. Benjamin B. Warfield, *The Person and Work of Christ* (Philadelphia: Presbyterian and Reformed, 1950), 574.

5. For a more detailed explanation, see Dr. Felix Asiedu's paper "The Example of a Woman: Sexual Renunciation and Augustine's Conversion to Christianity in 386," accessed July 25, 2012, http://www9.georgetown.edu/faculty/jod/augustine/felix.htm. The situation is more complex than I've described it. The church was confronted by the rampant sexual promiscuity in Roman culture. Door knockers in Pompeii were phallic symbols. Even barbarians (the Scythians, for example) were shocked by Roman pornography. In God's wisdom, it may have been that the only way to break the hold of this systemic corruption was to go "cold turkey" and embrace sexual abstention, as the medieval church did. Also, there were also enormous cultural pressures on Augustine to embrace celibacy. The mood of the church, including that of his pastor, Bishop Ambrose, denigrated marriage and exalted celibacy. St. Anthony, the celibate Egyptian monk, was the "rock star" of the fourth century.

Chapter 20. Wisdom in the Pursuit of Love

1. Frederic W. Bush, *Ruth, Esther*, Word Biblical Commentary (Nashville, TN: Thomas Nelson, 1996), 196–215. Because of our ignorance of ancient Israelite customs, there is a considerable ambiguity about this transaction. We don't understand the relationship between a *goel* and levirate marriage. We do know this: (1) In ancient Israel, all land belonged to God, and a family's land could never be sold permanently outside of the clan. (2) A *goel* could redeem the land for the family. (3) Boaz, as a *goel*, is now exercising his rights to redeem the land for Naomi. (4) There is a connection, not completely understood, between levirate marriage and land.

2. Bush, *Ruth, Esther*, 229–32. Bush dismisses the idea that So-and-So is the village idiot. But I think the weight of the evidence is for it. (1) The narrator has deliberately highlighted Boaz's "with-it-ness," and it makes for a striking contrast with So-and-So. (2) This view explains why the narrator would make a negative comment using his name. (3) It also creates a coherent picture of So-and-So. He is a biblical simpleton, a complete package of cluelessness, impetuosity, and greed—a complete contrast to Boaz's "with-it-ness," carefulness, and generosity. This view of Mr. So-and-So also explains as no one else has done to my satisfaction why Boaz withholds the information on Ruth. Bush's explanation (232,

244–45) that Boaz is calling So-and-So to his *moral* obligation to take care of Ruth doesn't fit what we know about village life. That would have been self-evident as soon as the negotiations began. Bush's explanation also rests on a series of inferences about levirate marriage. We simply do not know the interplay or obligations between levirate marriage, *goels*, and land.

3. This section is a new proposal that I've not seen in any of the literature. It makes sense of (1) suggestions in the text of So-and-So's character, (2) negotiating strategy in general, and finally (3) Boaz's holding off on playing his "Ruth" card." I've seen no other explanation that does justice to all three of these observations. Scholars tend to focus on literary clues and can neglect things like principles of negotiating.

4. Cynthia Ozick, *Metaphor and Memory* (New York: Vintage, 1991), 262–63.

Chapter 21. Love Celebrates

1. There are several clues in the text that Tamar might be a Canaanite. Judah has gone "down" (Canaanite territory) to lodge, and that is where he meets his Canaanite friend Hirah and where he marries a Canaanite wife. It looks like Judah remains in Canaanite territory because when he shears his sheep, he goes "up" (Israelite territory). Tamar hears this and goes "up" as well. All of this suggests that Tamar is a Canaanite. See Robert Alter, *The Five Books of Moses: A Translation with Commentary* (New York: Norton, 2004), 214–20.

2. There is much we don't know about levirate marriage, but the story of Tamar suggests that levirate marriage was a de facto obligation. That is, Judah and Tamar were functionally married. So Tamar's sexual intimacy with Judah was appropriate. Tamar's only recourse was to use deception to force Judah to be responsible. Deception in the Old Testament is a function of love and righteousness. So David at times deceives in order to spare his own life and others from evil.

3. Katharine Doob Sakenfeld, *Interpretation: A Bible Commentary for Preaching and Teaching: Ruth* (Louisville, KY: John Knox, 1999), 79.

4. Conversation with Dr. Steve Jamison who lived in Egypt with Dr. Ken Bailey. Dr. Jamison personally witnessed older Arab women wet-nursing babies.

Chapter 22. The Legacy of Love

1. Robert L. Hubbard Jr., *The Book of Ruth*, New International Commentary on the Old Testament (Grand Rapids: Eerdmans, 1988), 70.

2. Ibid., 275.

3. Daniel I. Block, *Judges, Ruth*, The New American Commentary (Nashville, TN: Broadman & Holman, 1999), 729.

4. Katharine Doob Sakenfeld, *Interpretation: A Bible Commentary for Preaching and Teaching: Ruth* (Louisville, KY: John Knox, 1999), 83.

5. Cynthia Ozick, *Metaphor and Memory* (New York: Vintage, 1991), 264.

6. Hubbard, *Book of Ruth*, 277.

7. It is difficult to date Ruth with certainty. The Hebrew is primarily Standard Biblical Hebrew—pre-exile date, but there are traces of Late Biblical Hebrew as well. The time of David and Solomon would be when the book would be most helpful functioning like a founding narrative. That also appears to be a kind of golden age of Hebrew literature. Ruth answers two potentially troubling questions for David: David's obscurity (What is David's lineage? Who is his family? Who does he think he is?) and rumors of Moabite roots to the family (His great-grandmother was a Moabite! How could he be king? He's not a true Israelite!).

8. Daniel I. Block, "Book of Ruth 1," in *Dictionary of the Old Testament: Wisdom, Poetry and Writings*, ed. Tremper Longman III and Peter Enns (Downers Grove, IL: IVP Academic, 2008), 682.

Chapter 23. Love Is Forever

1. Benjamin B. Warfield, *The Person and Work of Christ* (Philadelphia: Presbyterian and Reformed, 1950), 574.

WORKS CITED

Alter, Robert. *The Art of Biblical Narrative*. New York: Basic Books, 2011.

———. *The Five Books of Moses: A Translation with Commentary*. New York: Norton, 2004.

Asiedu, Felix. "The Example of a Woman: Sexual Renunciation and Augustine's Conversion to Christianity in 386." Accessed July 25, 2012. http://www9.georgetown.edu/faculty/jod/augustine/felix.htm.

Austin, Michael. "Achieving Happiness: Advice from Augustine." Accessed July 20, 2012. http://www.psychologytoday.com/blog/ethics-everyone/201106/achieving-happiness-advice-augustine.

Berlin, Adele. "The Book of Ruth." *Biblical Archaeology Review*. www.bib-arch/online-exclusives/ruth-1.asp.

Block, Daniel I. "Book of Ruth 1." In *Dictionary of the Old Testament: Wisdom, Poetry and Writings*, edited by Tremper Longman III and Peter Enns. Downers Grove, IL: IVP Academic, 2008.

———. *Judges, Ruth*. The New American Commentary. Nashville, TN: Broadman & Holman, 1999.

Bolick, Kate. "All the Single Ladies." *The Atlantic*, November 2011.

Bonhoeffer, Dietrich. *Letters and Papers from Prison*. New York: Touchstone, 1997.

Brooks, David. "It's Not About You." *New York Times*, May 30, 2011. Section A, 23.

Bunimovitz, Shlomo, and Avraham Faust. "Ideology in Stone: Understanding the Four-Room House." *Biblical Archaeology Review* 28, no. 4 (July/August 2002): 32–41.

Bush, Frederic W. *Ruth, Esther*. Word Biblical Commentary. Nashville, TN: Thomas Nelson, 1996.

Cahill, Thomas. *Desire of the Everlasting Hills*. New York: Doubleday, 1999.

Capper, Brian J. "Essene Community Houses and Jesus' Early Community." In *Jesus and Archaeology*, edited by James Charlesworth, 472–502. Grand Rapids: Eerdmans, 2006.

Chesterton, G. K. *Orthodoxy*. New York: Doubleday, 1959.

Coutu, Diane. "Putting Leaders on the Couch: A Conversation with Manfred F. R. Kets de Vries." *Harvard Business Review* 82, no. 1 (2004): 64–71.

Daviau, P. M. Michele, and Paul-Eugene Dion. "Moab Comes to Life." *Biblical Archaeology Review* 28, no. 1 (January/February 2002): 38–49, 63.

Dickinson, Emily. "Tell All the Truth, But Tell It Slant." Accessed February 19, 2013. http://www.canopicpublishing.com/poets/dickinsonTruth.htm.

Green, Douglas J. "Ruth Lectures." Class notes on the book of Ruth, a course taught at Westminster Theological Seminary.

Heraclitus. *Fragments: The Collected Wisdom of Heraclitus*. Translated by Brooks Haxton. New York: Viking, 2001.

Homan, Michael. "Did the Israelites Drink Beer?" *Biblical Archaeology Review* 36, no. 5 (September/October 2010): 48–56.

Hubbard, Robert L., Jr. *The Book of Ruth*. New International Commentary on the Old Testament. Grand Rapids: Eerdmans, 1988.

Irvin, B. P. "Ruth 3: History of Interpretation." In *Dictionary of the Old Testament: Wisdom, Poetry and Writings*, edited by Tremper Longman III and Peter Enns. Downers Grove, IL: IVP Academic, 2008.

Jay, Meg. "The Downside of Cohabiting before Marriage," *New York Times*, April 14, 2012. Section SR, 4.

Jenni, E., ed. *Theologisches Handwörterbuch zum Alten Testament*. Vol. 2. Munich: Kaiser, 1976.

Keller, Tim. "Absolutism: Don't We All Have to Find Truth for Ourselves?" Sermon delivered at Redeemer Presbyterian Church, New York, October 8, 2006.

———. "The Insider and the Outsider Encounter Jesus." Lecture delivered at the Oxford Inter-Collegiate Christian Union, Oxford University, February 8, 2012.

Lewis, C. S. *The Four Loves*. New York: Harcourt, Brace, 1988.

———. *Letters of C. S. Lewis*. Edited by W. H. Lewis. New York: Harcourt Brace Jovanovich, 1966.

———. *The Screwtape Letters*. New York: HarperCollins, 1996.

———. *Surprised by Joy*. New York: Harcourt Brace Jovanovich, 1966.

Marche, Stephen. "Is Facebook Making Us Lonely?" *The Atlantic*, May 2012.

Marsden, George M. *A Short Life of Jonathan Edwards*. Grand Rapids: Eerdmans, 2008.

Miller, Paul E. *Love Walked among Us: Learning to Love Like Jesus*. Colorado Springs: NavPress, 2001.

Ozick, Cynthia. "Ruth." In *Metaphor and Memory*. New York: Vantage, 1991.

Putnam, Fred. *A New Grammar of Biblical Hebrew*. Sheffield, UK: Sheffield Phoenix, 2010.

Rauber, Donald. "Literary Values in the Bible: The Book of Ruth." *Journal of Biblical Literature* 89, no. 1 (1970): 27–37.

Reno, R. R. "Postmodern Irony and Petronian Humanism." Mars Hill Audio Resources Essay. Vol. 67. March/April 2004.

Sakenfeld, Katharine Doob. *Interpretation: A Bible Commentary for Preaching and Teaching: Ruth*. Louisville, KY: John Knox, 1999.

Schwartz, Benjamin. "The Hitch." *The Atlantic*, March 2012.

Stott, John. *The Cross of Christ*. Downers Grove, IL: InterVarsity, 1986.

Trible, Phyllis. "A Human Comedy." In *God and the Rhetoric of Sexuality*, 166–99. Philadelphia: Fortress, 1978.

———. "Ruth 4: Person." In *Dictionary of the Old Testament: Wisdom, Poetry and Writings*, edited by Tremper Longman III and Peter Enns. Downers Grove, IL: IVP Academic, 2008.

Warfield, Benjamin B. *The Person and Work of Christ*. Philadelphia: Presbyterian and Reformed, 1950.

GENERAL INDEX

SCRIPTURE INDEX

170

A LOVING LIFE

A Loving Life: Interactive Bible Study
(NavPress)
by Paul E. Miller

A loving life is what we all want. But loving people is hard. This 17-lesson seeJesus interactive Bible study will help you share Ruth's amazing biblical portrait of love with a small group or Sunday school class. Here is the help we all need to embrace relationship, endure rejection, cultivate community, and reach out to even the most unlovable as we discover the power to live a loving life.

Leader and participant manuals available.

Excellent for small groups — and — Sunday school

"Here is love vast, unmeasured, boundless, free—and freeing."
–Bryan Chapell, President Emeritus, Covenant Theological Seminary; Senior Pastor, Grace Presbyterian Church, Peoria, IL

"The word 'love' is most often either a vague sentiment or just another four-letter word. But in Paul Miller's hands, the quiet, compelling reality emerges. You will witness how love is thoughtful, principled, enduring, and wise—all the things you know deep down it should be. And, even more than those fine things, you will be surprised and delighted at how true love is grounded in God." –David Powlison, Executive Director, Christian Counseling and Educational Foundation

"Through the biblical story of Ruth, Paul gives us hope, not hype—the freedom to suffer well, stay present, and live expectantly in all of our relationships." –Scotty Smith, Teacher-in-Residence, West End Community Church, Nashville, TN

**TO ORDER CALL 215.721.3113 OR
VISIT SEEJESUS.NET/STORE**

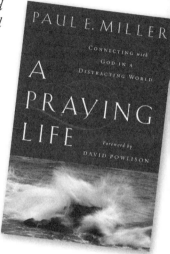

LOVE
WALKED
AMONG
US

Love Walked Among Us:
Learning to Love Like Jesus
(NavPress)
by Paul E. Miller

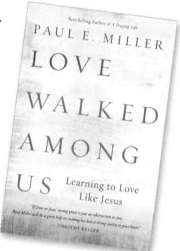

Paul Miller weaves together stories of his own struggles to love with stories of how Jesus loves. Your heart will be captured by the wonder of the person of Jesus. The book is based on the *Person of Jesus* study and, like the study, is written to introduce non-Christians to Jesus.

TO ORDER CALL 215.721.3113 OR
VISIT SEEJESUS.NET/STORE